a guide to

stress relief

Sara Rose

This is a Parragon Book

This edition published in 2002

Parragon
Queen Street House
4 Queen Street
Bath BA1 1HE, UK

ISBN: 0-75259-139-8

Printed in Italy

Designed and created with
The Bridgewater Book Company Ltd.

NOTE

Any information given in this book is not intended to be taken as a replacement for medical advice. Any person with a condition requiring medical attention should consult a qualified medical practitioner or therapist before beginning this or any other exercise programme.

Contents

Introduction

The definition of good health is a sense of well-being. But all too often we become caught up in a cycle of stress and strain that leaves us functioning below our best and feeling tired, anxious and unhappy. This book offers practical advice to help overcome the pressures of modern life, maintain health and regain vitality and peace of mind.

For long-term stress relief and optimum well-being you need periods of mental and physical relaxation throughout the day. Relaxation is a set of easily learned skills that will teach you how to combat the effects of stress and restore the balance between body and mind to enable healthy, happy living.

This book shows simple but effective ways of making relaxation an integral part of your everyday life. This opening section describes the detrimental effects of too much strain on the body and mind. It will help you identify the

Many people practise meditation techniques to achieve inner calm and improve their sense of well-being.

traits that can undermine well-being so that you can make changes in your life for the better. Two chapters deal with physical and mental relaxation, and describe natural ways of restoring the balance between mind and body, using a variety of techniques taken from Eastern and Western traditions. The final chapter covers lifestyle factors and environmental influences.

Reconnecting with the natural world is a particularly effective way of alleviating the pressures of modern living. A spectacular sunset can both rejuvenate and refresh the senses.

Many physical, mental and emotional problems can be avoided if you put just a little effort into looking after yourself in a more caring way. This practical guide gives easy-to-follow advice for long-term calm and serenity, to help you unwind and enjoy life to the full.

Stress: the problem

The increasing demands of modern life put enormous pressure on the mind and body. Some stress is part of life and is not necessarily a bad thing: it is a normal response to danger, and positive stress provides the spur to achieve. But when stress is long-term it can affect you physically, emotionally and spiritually, impacting on your well-being.

Causes of stress

There is an enormous spectrum of 'stressors' (causes of stress) – from the relatively routine ring of the telephone to something life-threatening such as a car crash. Major life events, such as moving home, birth, marriage, divorce or death; environmental factors, such as noise, flashing lights, overcrowding, pollution; lifestyle, including poor diet and lack of sleep and exercise – these are just some of the things that can contribute to stress. Your own temperament, constitution and previous experiences moderate the effects of stress but the more stressors there are, the less you are able to deal with them effectively.

The stages of adaptation

Stress has very definite physical effects but it sometime takes years for you to notice this. In the 1950s an American doctor, Hans Selye, identified three stages of adaptation in the human response to long-term stress.

1. Alarm response

Exposure to stressors prompts an immediate biochemical reaction known as the 'fight or flight' response. Stress hormones are released into the bloodstream, causing the following:

- increased heart rate and blood pressure
- raised blood-sugar and cholesterol levels
- faster breathing and perspiration
- increased muscle tension
- disruption of digestive processes
- suppression of the immune system
- emotional tension

Telephones ringing can amount to noise pollution and can, over time, cause a build-up of stress.

2. Adaptation

If the cause of stress is removed or dealt with, the body reverts to normal functioning, but if it continues the body copes by adapting. Although you may feel as though everything has returned to normal, your body uses up energy stores and over time this affects your ability to function efficiently, resulting in fatigue, irritability and lethargy.

3. Exhaustion

Long-term stress changes the balance of hormones in the body and leads to exhaustion. A suppressed immune system, slower metabolism and slower rate of cell repair results in rapid ageing, weight gain and a greater risk of degenerative disease. Your body becomes run down, with recurring minor illnesses and psychological 'burn-out'. Eventually you may become seriously ill or suffer a breakdown.

But although stress may cause a variety of disorders, it is not in itself an illness. Stress is created by habitual responses to difficult situations and by an unhealthy lifestyle. It is a habit that you can break, if you are prepared to look carefully at your life and take control.

A balanced body

Your body's biochemical, structural and psychological functions are delicately balanced to enable good physical and mental health, and an upset in any one area can lead to problems in others. Optimum health requires looking after all parts of the whole. A healthy body and a clear and active mind with a positive attitude will help you maintain this balance.

The body is an energy system that needs to keep balanced to function properly. Any kind of regular cardiovascular exercise – even walking – will keep the body in a healthy condition.

A strategy for relaxation

The key to relaxation is to be able to recognise when you are under too much pressure and then dedicate time to looking after yourself. Developing the ability to relax at will during times of intense pressure, as well as implementing long-term strategies for dealing with stress, will help you feel calmer and more in control of your life.

Benefits of relaxation

Relaxation can counter many of the effects of stress. Adrenaline levels decrease, reducing stress on the cardiovascular system and lowering blood pressure. Breathing becomes slower and more controlled. The muscles become less tense and digestive processes improve. The immune system becomes more active, making you less susceptible to illness.

Insomnia, coupled with constant tiredness, may be a sign that your immune system is under strain and that you need to change something in your life.

Recognising stress

The symptoms of stress generally manifest in behavioural, emotional and physical ways. If you regularly experience more than five of the following, you need to take action.

Behavioural:

- excessive drinking or smoking
- poor appetite or overeating
- avoiding others and an inability to enjoy company

Emotional:

- irritability, anger and readiness to explode for no apparent reason
- difficulties in decision-making, concentration or memory
- feelings of being overwhelmed and unable to cope
- depression
- tearfulness
- no sense of humour

Back or neck ache are two of the many ways that stress manifests itself.

Physical:

- constant tiredness
- insomnia
- clumsiness
- muscular aches and pains including backache and headaches
- skin problems
- high blood pressure
- palpitations and panic attacks
- breathing problems including asthma, shallow breathing and hyperventilation
- indigestion, heartburn, ulcers, nervous diarrhoea or constipation

You can't always avoid stress but being able to identify what causes it is the first step towards helping yourself cope better. In some cases you can take active steps to lead a calmer life – for example, if you find shopping stressful, why not order your groceries online instead?

Relaxation

Learn how to relax during times of great stress. Think of an activity that you associate with being calm, such as lying in the sun or having a warm bath. When you feel under pressure, think about your relaxation activity. Your mind will associate this with peace and you will soon start to feel relaxed.

On the record

Although you may recognise the symptoms of stress, it is sometimes difficult to pinpoint the cause. Keeping a record will help you to identify patterns of stress in your life.

1

Divide each page into sections, either an hourly breakdown, or for different times of the day (eg breakfast, morning, lunchtime, afternoon, evening).

2

Make a note of all your activities during the day and how you were feeling at the time.

3

Fill in your diary whenever a stress symptom occurs. If possible, make a note of what happened just before it occurred.

4

At the end of the week, evaluate the times when you felt stressed and when you felt relaxed.

	Monday	Tuesday	Wednesday	Thursday	Friday	Saturday	Sunday
Breakfast							
Morning							
Lunch							
Afternoon							
Evening							

PART 1: RELAXING YOUR BODY

Introduction

Efficient, controlled breathing and the ability to relax at will are vital in dealing effectively with stress. Simple breathing exercises and muscle relaxation techniques reduce the mental and physical effects of stress and enhance well-being. Touch and movement therapies benefit mind and body by increasing energy levels and engendering a sense of deep relaxation.

You can practise many different techniques originating from all over the world to enhance physical relaxation. You do not need to perform them all as part of your daily routine, but it is worth at least trying out as many as possible so that you can discover which are the most beneficial and comfortable for you. Some of these techniques normally depend on having a willing partner with you, but you can still reap the benefits of massage or reflexology by yourself.

Once you have found a range of relaxing exercises that suit you, it is important to develop a regular routine in the same way you would with any sport or exercise discipline. To see the true benefits you need to make it a part of your lifestyle rather than something that you do as a break from your routine. The small amount of time spent relaxing your body muscles and controlling your breathing each morning or evening will pay dividends over the rest of the day. Some people may find it more convenient to perform relaxing exercises in the evening, helping them unwind and preparing them for sleep. Should you do so, however, remember not to do any form of physical exercise straight after a meal or in the hours before going to bed.

Relaxed, controlled breathing exercises before you go to work in the morning will put you in the right mood for a successful day.

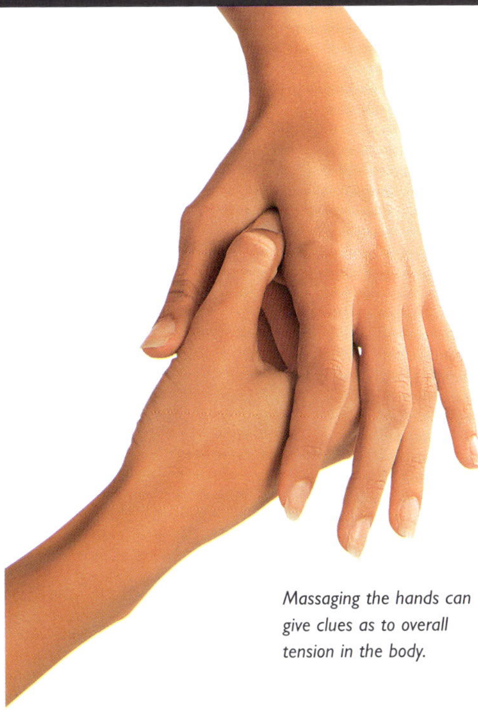

Massaging the hands can give clues as to overall tension in the body.

A space to relax

Just like any other form of physical exercise, your environment and clothing are as important as the routine you undertake. If at all possible, find a comfortable room that is without distractions – it will be far more difficult to relax if the television is on in the corner of the room. You should also be wearing loose-fitting clothing that allows you to move and breathe freely.

Although you should find that following a regular routine will provide you with a greater capacity to deal with stress in your day-to-day living, you will undoubtedly still be faced with unexpected crises at work or home. At such times you may find that taking a break to spend a few minutes working on your breathing or massaging yourself can put you in the right frame of mind to concentrate on finding a positive solution to the problem and so avoid being overwhelmed by the problem itself. Whichever routine you choose, it should improve your health and sense of well-being and help you deal with life's challenges more easily and with less stress.

This yoga position, a reversed Namaste *(Prayer pose) is good for stretching the shoulders and arm muscles and expanding the chest.*

Breathing

Correct breathing is the key to calming mind and body. How you breathe reflects your health and how you feel about yourself. Your breathing becomes shallow and rapid when you are anxious, but slow and deep when you are at ease. Years of stress and poor lifestyle means that rapid, shallow breathing is the norm for most of us.

Breathing is essential to life. As you breathe, oxygen is taken into the bloodstream and fuels the production of energy that enables your body to function. Breathing is an automatic, involuntary activity, but it can be consciously controlled. In times of acute stress, taking a minute to slow down and control your breathing will calm you instantly.

Correct, effective breathing should come from the deepest area of the lungs.

The effects of poor breathing

When stress levels rise, breathing tends to use only the top third of the lungs. There is a drop in levels of carbon dioxide, which is needed to maintain blood acidity, and harmful toxins are not breathed out. This has a direct detrimental effect on the nerves and muscles, and may result in tiredness, palpitations and panic attacks. If you learn to breathe properly, these conditions can be alleviated and you will also benefit from a lower heart-rate, reduced blood pressure and lower levels of stress hormones. So there are many benefits of learning to breathe correctly.

Breathing for health

Deeper breathing and a slower pulse are recognised signs of good health – the deeper the breath, the more body tissues can be oxygenated, and the stronger your heart is, the less often it needs to beat.

How to breathe

To improve your breathing you must first become aware of it. If you find your breathing is too fast or too shallow, the following exercise – known as abdominal breathing – will help you breathe more naturally. It uses the diaphragm (the sheet of muscle forming the top of the abdomen) to enable the lungs to inflate and deflate with minimal effort.

1

Sit in a comfortable position with your eyes open or closed. Place one hand on your chest and the other over your diaphragm just below the breastbone. Breathe in slowly through your nose, and try to breathe so that the hand on your chest remains relatively still.

2

Hold your breath for a few seconds then breathe out slowly through your nose. Release as much air as possible.

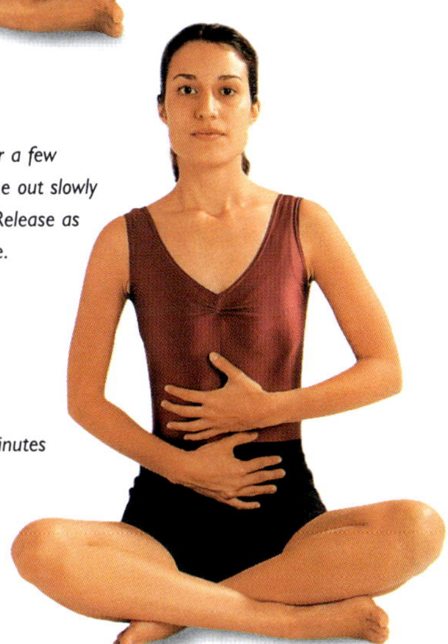

3

Repeat for a few minutes until you feel calm.

Alternate nostril breathing

Blow your nose to clear the nasal passages. Place your forefinger and second finger on your forehead, with the thumb and third finger on either side of your nose. Relax your thumb and inhale through that nostril then close with the thumb. Release your third finger and exhale through the other nostril. Continue to breathe in and out through alternate nostrils. This exercise helps you become aware of each breath, but stop if you feel dizzy.

Alternate nostril breathing can help you achieve mental balance and clarity.

Life force

Many Eastern philosophies believe that as well as containing oxygen, air also contains vital energy (known as *prana* in India, *qi* or *chi* in China and *ki* in Japan). By performing conscious breathing exercises you can accumulate this energy and revitalise both your mind and your body.

Reducing muscle tension

When your body and mind are under pressure, your muscles become constricted. Tight, cramped muscles restrict the body's blood supply, causing pain, fatigue and tension. Over-tense muscles can dramatically affect your posture, movement, and body functioning. To relax, you must first locate the tension and try to release it.

Progressive muscle relaxation

This relaxation technique, which tenses and releases all the major muscle groups, will help you to slow down and let go of muscle tension. Choose a quiet time of day when you will not be disturbed.

1

Remove your shoes and loosen tight clothing. Lie on a mat on the floor or a firm bed, with a pillow under your head for support. Close your eyes and focus on breathing slowly, emphasising the out-breath.

2

Tense the muscles in your right foot, hold for a few seconds then release. Tense and release the calf, then the thigh muscles. Repeat with the left foot and leg.

3

Tense and release the muscles in your right hand and arm, then the left.

4

Tense and release each buttock, then the stomach muscles.

5

Lift your shoulders up to your ears, hold for a few seconds, then lower. Repeat three times. Rock your head gently from side to side.

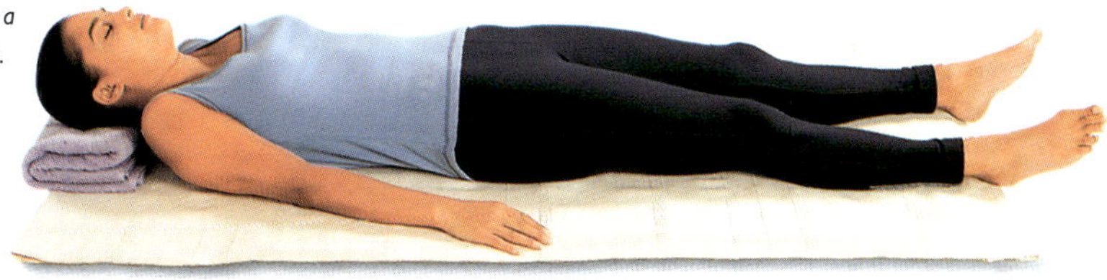

6

Yawn, then pout. Frown, wrinkle your nose and let go. Raise your eyebrows then relax your face muscles.

7

Focus on your breathing again. Wriggle your fingers and toes, bend your knees and gently roll on to your side, then get up slowly.

Alexander technique

This method of self-awareness, devised by an Australian actor, aims to improve balance, posture and coordination so that the body can operate with minimum strain. By learning to stand and move correctly, you can alleviate muscular tension and enable the body systems to function more efficiently.

The technique consists of three stages: releasing unwanted tension; learning new ways of moving, standing or sitting; and learning new ways of reacting physically and mentally to various situations. It should be learned from a qualified teacher and practised regularly.

Flotation and water therapy

Flotation tanks are sound-proofed tanks of warm water in which salts and minerals have been dissolved to enable the body to float effortlessly. This is a way of isolating body and mind from external stimuli in order to induce deep relaxation. During flotation the body and mind become profoundly relaxed and the brain releases endorphins, natural painkillers.

Hot water dilates blood vessels, reducing blood pressure. For a simple home remedy to relax stiff muscles, soak in a warm bath.

Massage

Using touch is a very effective way of becoming relaxed, and massage is one of the easiest and most reliable ways of relieving stress and relaxing painful muscles. This soothing therapy releases tension and reduces anxiety. There are numerous kinds of massage, many of which have been incorporated into various complementary therapies.

Physical effects of massage

Gentle massage stimulates sensory nerve endings in the skin, which transmit messages through the nervous system to the brain. The brain responds by releasing endorphins, natural painkillers that induce a feeling of well-being. Massage further aids relaxation by affecting the body systems that control blood pressure, heart rate, digestion and breathing, resulting in increased health.

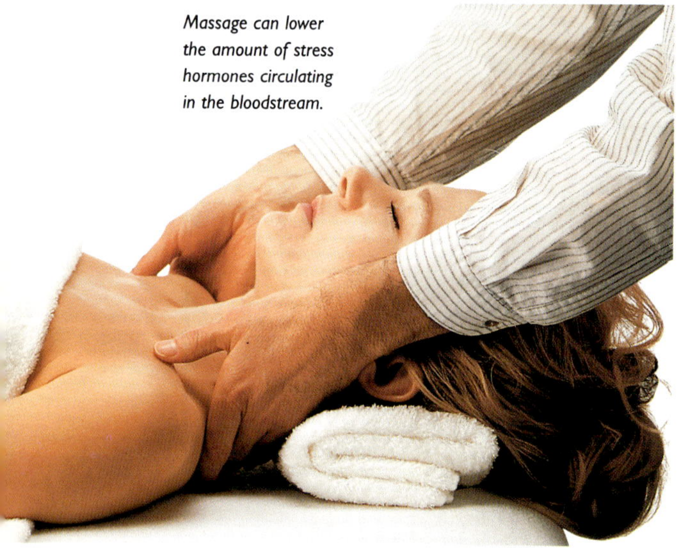

Massage can lower the amount of stress hormones circulating in the bloodstream.

Neck and shoulder massage

Tense, aching muscles are usually felt in the neck and shoulders. When you are tired, your posture tends to slump, straining your neck and shoulder muscles. It is extremely relaxing to have someone massage your neck and shoulders, but you can easily massage yourself.

Receiving massage

Make sure the room is warm and comfortable, then undress and lie down. Your partner should warm his or her hands then place a few drops of massage oil into the palms and knead the skin around your shoulder blades for a few minutes. Your partner can then place his or her hands between the tops of the shoulder blades and rotate the thumbs to massage lightly down the sides of the spine (not pressing on the bones) and along the shoulder blades. Your partner can finish the massage by squeezing the shoulder muscles to release deep-seated tension.

Self-massage

Shrug your shoulders and push them back as far as possible. Hold for five seconds then release. Repeat five times. Put your hand at the top of your arm and knead the flesh firmly, moving slowly towards your neck. Repeat three times. Press your fingers into the back of your neck and move the fingertips in a circular motion towards the base of the skull. Repeat five times. Holding the back of your head, rotate your thumbs at the base of your skull.

Quick fixes for headaches

Smooth the tips of your fingers over your forehead, working from the centre to the temples. Now place your palm on your forehead with your fingers pointing horizontally and gently move it up towards your hairline. Repeat with the other hand and continue until the tension ebbs away.

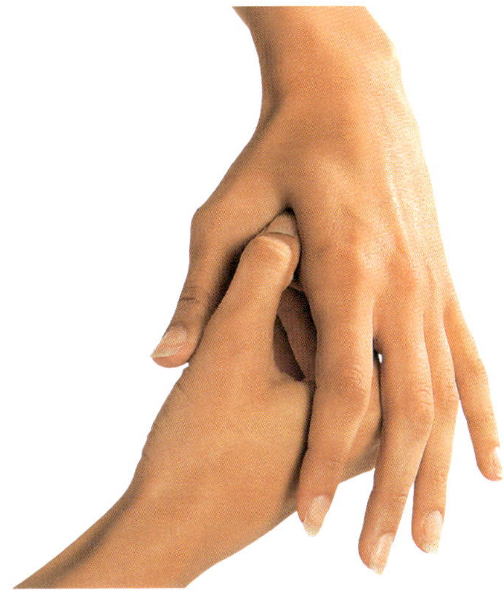

Regular hand massage can help relieve joint problems and arthritis.

Hand massage

Massage the web between your thumb and forefinger, using the opposite hand to press as close as possible to the point where the two bones meet. Continue for about a minute then repeat on the other hand. This is a technique employed in acupressure, an ancient Chinese form of massage and healing.

Caution

Do not massage swellings, fractures, bruises or infected skin. The stomach, legs and feet should not be massaged in the first trimester of pregnancy. If you suffer from varicose veins, back pain or thrombosis, seek professional medical advice before having any massage treatment.

Restoring vital energy

Every day we accumulate stress, which is stored in our minds as anxiety and in our bodies as tension. Many philosophies hold that tension blocks the flow of vital energy and prevents us from being rejuvenated. Therapies that unblock this tension have been devised to restore your body's state of equilibrium.

Yoga

Yoga has been practised in India for thousands of years and is now popular around the world. There are many types of yoga but the form most common in the West is 'hatha' yoga, which means balance of mind and body. This comprises body postures (*asanas*) and breathing techniques (*pranayama*) to prepare the body so that the mind can meditate without obstructions or obstacles.

Breathing correctly is the key to hatha yoga, and when done properly every movement is coordinated with the breath. Each *asana* is designed to stretch and strengthen the body, and is generally held for between 20 seconds and two minutes.

Everyone can practise yoga, regardless of fitness or age, but when learning it is advisable to attend classes held by a qualified teacher. Regular daily practice will increase energy and stamina, tone muscles, improve digestion and concentration, and help you relax and deal with life's daily stresses.

Natarajasana, *or the Dancer position, helps strengthen the muscles in the legs, feet and lower back, as well as improving balance.*

Precautions

If you suffer from back pain, high blood pressure, or heart disease, or if you are pregnant, consult your doctor before starting a new exercise regime. When practising yoga, certain postures such as headstands should be avoided during pregnancy or menstruation and others are not suitable if you have certain medical conditions – consult your yoga teacher first.

The physical benefits of the ancient Chinese practice of T'ai Chi *include toned and strengthened muscles, more efficient internal organs, improved posture and increased circulation.*

T'ai Chi

This ancient Chinese martial art uses sequences of slow, graceful movements and breathing techniques to relax mind and body. *T'ai Chi* exercises aim to restore the balance of *qi* and enhance health and vitality.

Flow of *qi*

Ancient Chinese philosophy teaches the concept of *yin* and *yang*, opposite but complementary forces whose balance within the body is essential for well-being. The interaction of *yin* and *yang* gives rise to *qi* or *chi*, an invisible 'life force' that flows around the body. The free circulation of *qi* is vital for good health: illness is thought to be caused by a blockage of *qi*.

Reflexology

Foot and hand massage have long been used to promote relaxation and improve health. The hands and feet are considered to be a mirror of the body and pressure on specific reflex points is thought to affect corresponding body parts. Reflexologists believe that granular deposits accumulate around reflex points, blocking energy flow, and the aim is to break down these deposits and improve the blood supply to flush away toxins.

Reflexology is generally performed on the feet by a trained practitioner and is deeply relaxing, but you can easily massage your hands at any time to relieve stress.

When pain, discomfort or illness is found somewhere in the body, a good reflexologist can use reflexology maps of the feet to discover which part of the foot should be treated.

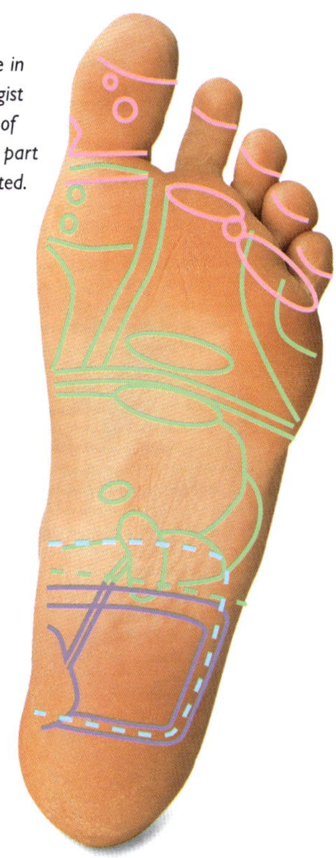

PART 2: RELAXING MIND AND SPIRIT

Introduction

Your thoughts, moods, emotions and beliefs have a fundamental impact on your basic health, healing mechanisms and immune system. To be truly healthy you need to look after your mind as well as your body. There are many different types of mind therapies designed for mental relaxation and to reverse the stress response. To a certain extent the type of person you are will determine how you react to a stressful event, but there are techniques you can learn to improve your self-image that will give you the ability to cope better with life's many challenges and difficulties.

The techniques described in this section, such as meditation and visualisation, offer ways of relaxing your mind so that you can control its responses to stress, and also enable you to change the way you think about yourself and the challenges that you face.

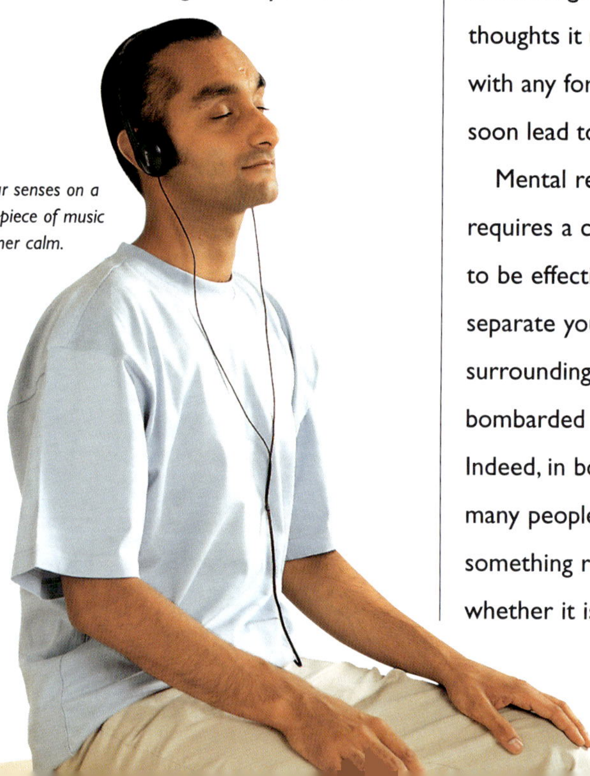

Focus your senses on a favourite piece of music to find inner calm.

Know your mind

Relaxing your mind is the natural complement to relaxing your body, and to be able to deal with stress you need to master your ability to do both. For those who are not used to meditating and other forms of controlling their thoughts it may not feel natural at first but, as with any form of exercise, regular practice will soon lead to it becoming second nature.

Mental relaxation, like physical relaxation, requires a calm and comfortable environment to be effective, and you will find it far easier to separate your mind from your immediate surroundings if your senses are not being bombarded by the bustle of life around you. Indeed, in both meditation and visualisation, many people find it easier if they have something relaxing to focus their senses on, whether it is peaceful music, images of a beautiful, calming scene or a favourite aroma. These need not be physically present – even the memories of such sensations can help you to relax and take control of your mind.

As you become more experienced in controlling your mind's reactions, however, you may find that you are able to switch to a relaxed state despite the distractions around you, a situation that has obvious benefits for dealing with stressful situations.

Along with the need to relax your mind and control its responses to stress, the need to change the way you think about yourself and your life is important. Few people realise the destructive impact on their lives of thinking about what they haven't achieved, the unattainable goals they set themselves or even negative things that have not yet occurred. Learning to think about what you have achieved and setting realistic goals is a valuable way of avoiding generating unnecessary stress.

Mental relaxation is not based on purely internal factors, however, and relationships with other people can provide happiness and calm in your daily life and support in the most difficult of times. Developing and strengthening your relationships with family and friends is also vital to achieving inner calm.

Visualising a favourite place can help you achieve a positive frame of mind in the most trying of times.

Meditation

Meditation is an effective way of focusing your mind to bring about relaxation, peace and tranquillity. It will help you to gain a new perspective and enable you to stand back from your problems. Meditation is often practised as a means of spiritual self-enlightenment, but it can also be used to relieve stress and promote relaxation.

What is meditation?

There are various types of meditation but they all focus on quietening the mind. The intention is to direct your concentration so that it is filled with peace and calm and cannot take off on its own and become stressed. When the mind is calm and focused in the present it is neither reacting to memories nor worrying over the future, two major sources of chronic stress. Meditation techniques can be divided into two basic groups:

Meditation is a practical and effective way of dealing with stress.

1. Concentrative meditation

This focuses your attention on something specific, such as the intake of breath, or an image or a phrase, in order to still the mind and facilitate the emergence of a greater awareness and clarity.

2. 'Mindfulness' meditation

Also known as *vipassana*, or 'passive awareness', this describes a state of mind where you are aware of, but detached from, everything you are experiencing. Your attention is aware of sensations, feelings, images, thoughts and sounds without thinking about them; you observe without making judgements. This means experiencing what happens in the here and now to gain a calmer, clearer and non-reactive state of mind. If you use the analogy of a camera, it is like looking through a wide-angle lens – you experience more and your attention becomes broader.

Meditation and the brain

The brain is the body's computer, the centre of all our thoughts, feelings and sensory experiences, and the coordinator of all our bodily functions. The brain sends and receives messages via the spinal cord to all parts of the body. Brain cells communicate with each other by producing tiny electrical impulses. Meditation affects the electrical activity of the brain, causing the production of high-intensity alpha waves – brain waves associated with deep relaxation and mental alertness. These in turn help to undermine our habitual stressed responses to dangers and difficulties.

During alpha-wave states the part of the nervous system that governs automatic body functions – such as breathing, perspiration, salivation, digestion and heart rate – predominates, reversing the 'fight-or-flight' response to danger and stress.

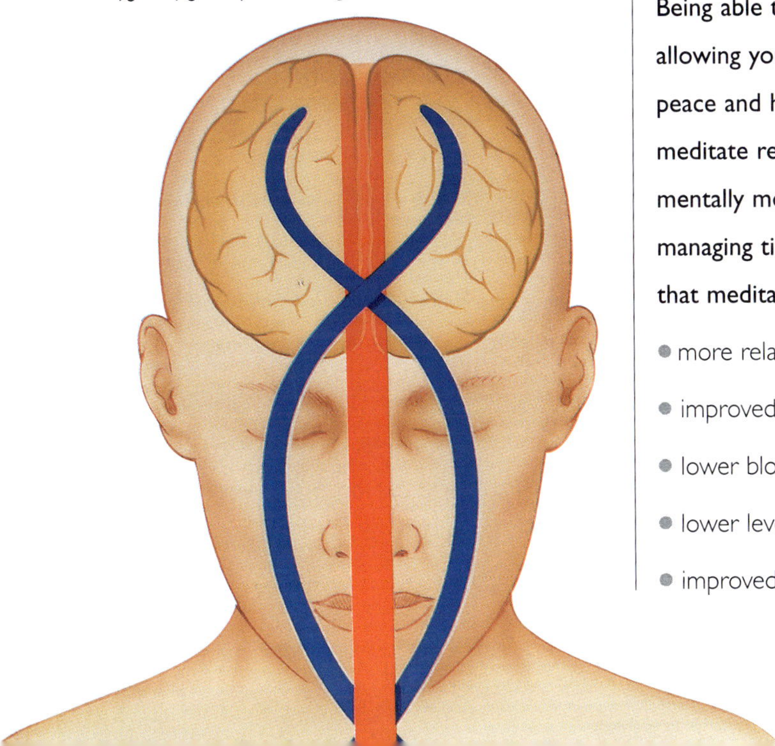

The brain produces four types of brain waves, which indicate our physical state: alpha (when we are deeply relaxed), beta (awake), delta (during a state of deep sleep) and theta (light sleep).

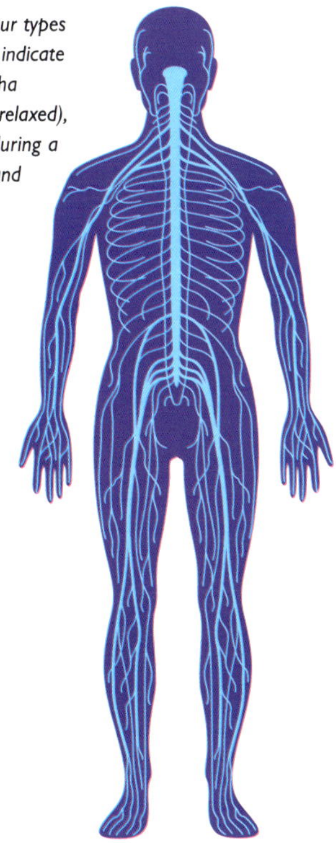

The benefits of meditation

Being able to control your mind instead of allowing your mind to control you will bring peace and harmony into your life. Those who meditate regularly are less anxious, calmer, mentally more alert and more efficient in managing time and energy. Research suggests that meditation confers the following benefits:

- more relaxed body
- improved sleeping patterns
- lower blood pressure and reduced pulse rate
- lower levels of stress hormones in the blood
- improved circulation

How to meditate

It helps to consult a teacher who can show you how to achieve a meditative state but you can teach yourself if you are sufficiently disciplined. There is no 'right' way to meditate but in order to do so successfully there are a few basic requirements to follow.

- a quiet place where you will not be disturbed
- regular practice, preferably for 15 minutes a day at the same time of day – meditation in the morning helps you to feel calm and centred for the rest of the day; meditation at night allows you to wind down
- an empty stomach
- a comfortable position (usually sitting to stop you from falling asleep)
- a focus for the mind to help you withdraw from your environment

Household items, such as a plant, candle or picture, can provide a focus for object-centred meditation.

Focusing the mind

You may find it difficult to concentrate at first, but this will improve with practice. You may also feel sleepy to begin with but as you meditate for longer you will feel more alert. If you feel your attention wandering, just bring it back to the focus of meditation. People usually achieve a meditative state by one of the following methods:

Using an object such as a flower for meditation can help keep the mind concentrated and attention focused.

Object meditation

Concentrate on a particular object, feeling its presence and focusing on its texture, shape and other qualities. A crystal, a candle flame, a flower or a mandala (a picture with a focal point) are all suitable objects.

Chanting a mantra or phrase, such as the sacred 'om', can help you maintain concentration and meditate successfully.

Mantra meditation

A 'mantra' is a word or phrase repeated continually, either silently or aloud. The Hindu 'aum' or 'om' is a sacred mantra that is widely used, though any word could be suitable.

Touch

Rhythmically passing a rosary or worry beads through the fingers, or rubbing a piece of fabric, can induce a state of meditation.

Breath awareness

Focus on your breathing to achieve a state of meditation. Count 'one' on each out-breath.

Active meditation

Rhythmic exercise such as *T'ai Chi*, swimming or walking can focus the mind and are more energising than sitting still.

Exercise: Quick and easy meditation

1

Sit comfortably with your spine straight. Look downwards, but not focusing on anything.

2

Let your eyelids drop to a level that feels comfortable without closing your eyes completely.

3

Continue to look downwards. You should notice that your breathing is slower and deeper.

4

Return your eyes to their normal focus after a couple of minutes. You should feel relaxed and calm.

Caution

Consult your doctor before starting meditation if you have a history of psychiatric disorders. Long-term meditation sometimes causes depression and withdrawal.

Visualisation

Visualisation, a technique that harnesses the imagination to deal with stress and illness, improve motivation and change negative attitudes, is an important part of many relaxation therapies, and is used by athletes. Through imagining sights, sounds, tastes or smells, you can use positive thinking to restore and maintain good health.

Self-help

Although you can consult a professional teacher to learn visualisation, it is possible to learn the technique on your own. At first, you will probably need to practise for 15–20 minutes a day, either first thing in the morning or last thing at night, but as you become more skilled you should be able to do it for just a few minutes at a time as needed.

Choose a quiet, comfortable place where you won't be disturbed. Breathe slowly and try to relax your body. Then focus on your chosen image. It helps to repeat positive affirmations as you do this, such as 'I feel relaxed' or 'I am in control'. You can perform this exercise in times of stress and it will help you gain control of a difficult or challenging situation.

Now visualise a calm, beautiful scene, real or imaginary, to help you relax. Suitable images include a peaceful garden, a beach, or a room. Try to envisage the sounds, smells and sights of the scene and soak up the atmosphere until you feel truly relaxed.

Visualising a calm, serene scene, such as a deserted sandy beach, is an effective way of using the imagination to help you relax and overcome stress and anxiety.

Fear of situations

Most people experience some degree of nerves or panic before important occasions, but visualisation can help you feel more in control. For example, for several days before the event, anticipate dealing successfully with a job interview, or imagine the round of applause after public speaking, and the affirmation will take root in your subconscious.

Imagery can also be used to overcome stress. Think of an image that you associate with tension (such as a thunderstorm) and replace it with something calming (a rainbow).

Powerful, tense scenes – such as a thunderstorm – can be imagined and replaced with something calming, like a rainbow, to help induce inner calm.

Colour visualisation

Colour can have a profound effect on your mood, vitality and well-being. Yellows and reds are stimulating: blues and greens calming. Colour therapists use different colours to improve your physical, emotional and spiritual health, generally by shining coloured lights onto your body. This exercise uses colour visualisation to calm the mind and help you relax.

1

Sit comfortably with your eyes closed.

2

Imagine a ball of golden light just above your head. Visualise the ball of light slowly descending through your head until it fills your entire body. Imagine that this light is cleansing and healing your spirit.

3

Repeat, visualising a ball of red light. Continue slowly through the colour spectrum – orange, yellow, green, blue, indigo and violet – until you feel completely relaxed.

The sound of crashing waves can be soothing, helping you to relieve stress and create inner calm.

Music and sounds

The therapeutic potential of music and sounds has long been recognised. Sound waves vibrate at different frequencies and have emotional and physical results, affecting your moods, heart rate, breathing and even prompting the release of endorphins. Whether or not you can sing in tune, the very act of singing releases tension and encourages you to breathe deeply and rhythmically. Making or responding to music can connect you directly to your inner self, enabling you to express profound emotions. Soft, quiet music will calm you down, while loud music stirs the soul.

A relaxation tape

Making your own relaxation tape is much more effective than buying one off the shelf. Choose a gentle, relaxing piece of music, lasting for at least 10 minutes, that you associate with pleasant memories. Add some sounds of nature if you like (for example, birdsong, a breeze rustling through the trees, or sounds of the sea).

Choose a quiet room to relax in, sit or lie down, close your eyes and play the tape. Try to match the rhythm of your breathing to that of the music, and conjure up pleasant mental images as you do so. Listen to the tape once a day if possible, and soon you will be able to use the memory of this music to calm you down in times of stress.

Release healing endorphins by listening to your favourite music or sounds from nature.

Therapeutic touch

One of the surest ways of soothing stress is through touch. However, physical contact does not have to be sexual. Stroking a cat or giving someone a hug can be just as effective. For a quick relief from stress, sit quietly for a moment with your index finger touching the thumb of the same hand. Massage is another tried and tested way of relaxing and alleviating stress (see pages 16–17).

Sense of smell

Different aromas can lift your mood and make you feel much better about yourself. Smell molecules travel along the olfactory pathways and directly into the limbic system, which is the part of the brain that controls memories, instincts and vital functions. For this reason, some smells are intensely evocative and can conjure up vivid scenes from nearly forgotten memories. Fragrant aromatherapy oils are used in a number of ways to aid relaxation (see pages 58–59).

You can also use the memory of scent and its powers of association to help you stay calm and relaxed during times of stress. Think about your favourite smells – a baby's skin, freshly ground coffee, oranges, the smell of frying bacon, your favourite flowers, new-mown grass – and you will instantly feel happier, more carefree and more relaxed.

Aromatherapy oils and the scent of joss sticks can be relaxing to the mind and body.

Creative relaxation

Creative activities such as painting, drawing and sculpting are excellent outlets for your emotions and can be deeply relaxing. Talent is not an issue – you do not need to produce a 'good' work of art. The mere act of performing an activity that is creative rather than a chore is relaxing in itself. Let yourself become aware of the different textures and aromas of the art media you are using – whether paints, crayons, chalks or clay – and enjoy the experience.

Visiting an art gallery can also be relaxing, particularly if you find a favourite picture or painting that has special associations for you. Go during a quiet time of day when you can sit and contemplate a piece without being disturbed.

More techniques for mind control

There are several other mind techniques you can be taught to reverse the body's stress response, including hypnotherapy, autogenic training and biofeedback. All these will help you relax and take control of your life.

Hypnotherapy

A hypnotic trance is a state of consciousness similar to daydreaming, which can be used to change patterns of behaviour and promote positive thinking. While you are in a hypnotic state you are very relaxed and open to suggestions. One theory to explain this is that under hypnosis the conscious, rational part of the brain is bypassed (the left hemisphere) and the subconscious, non-analytical part (the right hemisphere) takes over. During hypnosis the practitioner may 'feed' suggestions to your subconscious mind to overcome a specific problem, such as nicotine addiction or lack of confidence; or he or she might ask about past experiences to analyse current problems. A hypnotherapist can take you into a state of deep relaxation, which you may be able to recreate when faced with stressful situations.

Self-hypnosis

Most people can learn to hypnotise themselves. Find a place where you are unlikely to be disturbed and sit quietly or lie down. Relax and breathe slowly and deeply. Close your eyes and imagine yourself walking down a country lane, or descending a staircase, counting down from ten to zero as you go. Repeat positive affirmations to deal with your problem, or listen to a prerecorded tape of yourself. Bring yourself out of hypnosis by reversing the method with which you entered the hypnotic state.

To fully relax and go into a state of hypnosis, the mind has to envisage a quiet place, such as a country lane or a tranquil sky.

Caution

Hypnotherapy and autogenic training can be harmful to those who suffer from disorders such as severe depression, psychosis or epilepsy. Always consult a qualified and reputable practitioner.

Autogenic training

Autogenic means 'generated from within' and describes the way in which your mind can influence your body to train your autonomic nervous system – the part of the brain that governs automatic body functions – to become relaxed. Autogenic training (AT) consists of six silent mental exercises that enable you to switch off the body's stress response at will. With practice you should reach an altered state of consciousness known as 'passive concentration', a state of awareness similar to meditation whereby you relax by not actively working to do so.

Autogenic training seems to work best when performed in a sequence and with set phrases, such as 'my right arm is heavy, my left arm is heavy, both of my arms are heavy'. Each exercise is designed to relax different areas of the body. Once learned, the technique can be practised at home. AT needs to be performed on a regular basis to maintain the technique and ensure its continued effectiveness.

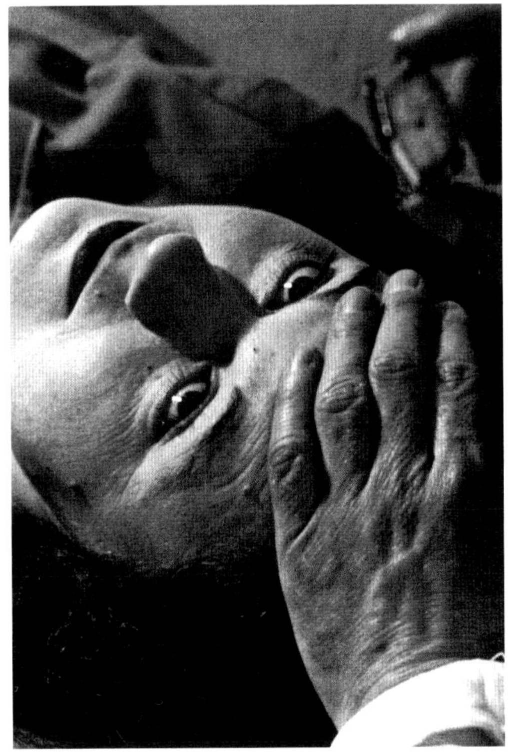

When in a state of hypnosis, the mind is very relaxed and open to suggestions, offering hypnotherapists the opportunity to replace negative thoughts and associations with positive ones.

Biofeedback

Biofeedback is a way of monitoring and controlling unconscious biological functions through electronic devices. It can also help you monitor your response to stress. Probes or electrodes are attached to your body and connected to electronic 'biofeedback' instruments that monitor physical responses. While getting feedback you perform relaxation exercises to regulate body functions until you reach a state of relaxation.

A sense of self

How you feel about yourself is key to becoming relaxed and overcoming stress. Anything you can do to sustain a more positive frame of mind will be beneficial to your physical health. You need to be confident about who you are and what you want to achieve – this will help you successfully manage your life and your relationships.

Improving self-worth

It is all too easy to belittle your own abilities and achievements, and most of us regularly make negative statements about ourselves without even realising it. But if you value yourself and your positive attributes, other people will value you as well.

Pioneered in the 1920s by French pharmacist Emile Coué, autosuggestion is a simple but effective technique that can change the way you think about yourself and the way you react to others. It consists of repeating simple, positive statements, made in the present tense, such as 'Every day, in every way, I am getting better and better'. Autosuggestion is most effective when you use preplanned and memorised phrases as a part of meditation or visualisation.

Improve your self-worth by affirming your good characteristics and repeating positive statements to yourself.

Set yourself attainable life goals – write a plan or a series of steps to move toward them.

Setting goals

Change is inevitable and desirable, but can be deeply unnerving as it pushes us out into the unknown. When contemplating long-term, positive change, it will help you on your way to identify some short-term, attainable goals. First you need to think of goals you would like to achieve in different areas of your life – relationships, work, money matters, healthy lifestyle, for example – within a specific time frame; but these need to be realistic, and don't try to change too much at once. Write them down and think of at least three steps you can take to reach each one. Reward yourself after each step on the way. If a particular goal seems unattainable, perhaps you need to give yourself more steps to reach it, or maybe you are simply being unrealistic and need to modify what you are trying to achieve.

Going with the flow

In order to stay relaxed you have to accept that you only have control over your own actions. Fighting to control the world around you is exhausting and often unsuccessful. But if you accept that life is full of obstacles, they become easier to deal with.

Laughing it off

As well as being fun, laughing gives the heart and lungs a good workout, and research indicates that it also lowers blood pressure, relaxes muscles, reduces pain, reduces stress hormones, and boosts the immune system by increasing the production of disease-destroying cells. Laughter triggers the release of endorphins, the body's natural painkiller, and produces a general sense of well-being.

Living for the moment

Small children have a wonderful facility for enjoying the moment, because they are free of the heavy burden of the past and have not yet learned to fear the future. As adults we are so conditioned to think of a hundred things at once that we often find it difficult to break free and just 'be' in the here and now. Many Eastern philosophies incorporate the idea of 'mindfulness' – being acutely aware of the present by keeping the mind fully absorbed in the task you are performing.

Mindfulness is a technique that can be learned, although it takes practice to stop your attention from wandering. Next time you have to perform an unwelcome task (such as doing the ironing), instead of daydreaming, concentrate fully on the job in hand. Focus on the rhythmic movement of your chore. When you become fully involved in the moment, even the most mundane tasks can focus your mind, helping you to feel calm and centred.

Performing everyday tasks, such as washing up the dishes, can help you achieve mindfulness. Concentrate fully on the job in hand.

Positive commuting

Negative feelings sap your energy and set up a self-perpetuating cycle of disappointment, worry and regret. Positive thinking gives you hope, and once set into motion you will feel better about many aspects of your life.

With practice you can change negative thoughts into positive ones. Think of an activity you find stressful – for example, commuting to work each day. Start by focusing on the downside (the wasted time, or the tiredness induced by a long journey). Tell these thoughts to go away. Consciously switch your negative thoughts to positive ones – think of using the time spent commuting to read, meditate or listen to music.

With practice, it can become second nature to think of the positive things in life, rather than the negative.

Count your blessings

Competition and striving for material success causes much of the stress in our society, and it is all too easy to forget the truly important things in life. Take a few moments each day to think carefully about the good things you have. These can be anything – good relationships, special skills, good health or happy children. Forget about competing for more things and feel at peace with yourself.

Freedom from fear

No one can be absolutely certain what lies ahead and often fear of what the future may hold prevents our enjoyment of the present. Instead of thinking about the what ifs? (what if I lose my job/become ill/can't pay my mortgage, for example), stop worrying and enjoy what you have at the moment. Visualisation exercises, which enable you to create an image of the future as you want it to be, are particularly beneficial in helping you to look forward to the future, rather than dreading it, but again this should be something achievable and not just a fantasy. You may find it helps to dedicate a certain time of day for thinking about your worries. When the time is up, just stop thinking about them.

Relationships

Maintaining good relationships with family and friends gives you emotional support and makes you feel more positive, thus reducing stress levels and engendering calm. All relationships need to be worked at, so that everyone feels valued and loved.

Improving your relationships

Learn to listen to what others have to say and in return they will respond to you. Practise kindness, tolerance, forgiveness and trust. Confide in your friends or family, and tell them how you are feeling.

Friends

For many people in the Western world, it is friends rather than family who provide emotional support, and just as we sometimes do with family members, we often take friends for granted. It is important to make time to show your appreciation for your friends, and to reflect upon the benefits they bring.

When spending time with your partner, burning aromatic candles can be a perfect way to create an intimate atmosphere.

Partners

Successful adult partnerships provide support, security and fulfilment, and physical and emotional communication is essential for a stress-free relationship. To make the most of your partnership it is vital to take time to be with each other. To promote intimacy in your relationship, try the following:

- Establish the mood by lighting candles and playing soft, relaxing music.
- Add aphrodisiac essential oils such as ylang ylang or jasmine to a massage oil, and give each other a sensual, soothing massage.
- Add essential oils to a warm bath, or burn in a vaporiser in the bedroom to give it a sensual scent.
- Take a relaxing bath together.
- Talk about the good things in your life, and plans for the future.

Take time to enjoy your children; play with them, and their enthusiasm and vitality will rub off on you.

Discussion

Relationships are much more open and fulfiling if you are honest with each other about your problems and needs. But you still need to maintain a degree of tact and try to avoid hurtful statements and actions.

- Set aside a time for discussion, but reschedule if either of you is tired, stressed or has had too much to drink.
- Think carefully about what you want to say beforehand – jot down a list of points you want to discuss.
- Try to be positive rather than focusing on the negative aspects of a situation.
- Don't hold your discussions in the bedroom, especially just before you are going to sleep, and avoid using a room where you would usually relax – you may even prefer to go for a walk, away from the home.
- Once you have reached an agreed conclusion, reaffirm your love for each other.

Children

Children are physically, emotionally and financially draining. However, they are also an endless source of pleasure and unconditional love, and they grow up all too quickly.

Bereavement

The death of a loved one is a source of profound stress. Grief increases your susceptibility to illness and diminishes your ability to cope. Grieving is a process that passes through various stages, including shock, denial, anger and finally acceptance. Expressing your emotions will prevent you from becoming overwhelmed by grief.

When grieving, don't bottle up your emotions – this will only prolong the pain and could lead to mental health problems.

PART 3: LIFESTYLE AND ENVIRONMENT

Introduction

Just a few simple adjustments to your lifestyle and environment can reap untold benefits for your general health and vitality. Making these changes is part of the process of taking more care of yourself. By organising your work and leisure more effectively, you will feel on top of your problems and in control of your life.

While relaxing our minds teaches us to appreciate the present and not to worry unduly about the future, it does not mean that we should not think about the day ahead of us. It is common not to take stock of how we live in the short- to medium-term, yet spending a little time to plan the day or the week ahead can make a big difference to how healthy our lifestyle is, both physically and mentally. One of the most fundamental changes we can make to improve our well-being is to our diet; making a record of what you consume over a few days can be a real eye-opener and balancing your diet should be a priority. The changes may feel strange at first, but the benefits to your life should soon become apparent and the alterations will soon cease to seem like sacrifices.

The amount of exercise that people undertake in the developed world is far below what is considered a healthy level for an adult, yet it is surprising how easy it can be to incorporate an effective amount into your daily routine. As well as exercises that you can perform in the morning or early evening, most people will find it easy to incorporate more walking in their working day, for example.

With work being one of the most common causes of stress in our lives, it is not surprising that it is also one of the most fruitful areas for change, from the moment your alarm goes off in the morning to the time you return home in the evening. Paradoxically, planning short breaks at work and knowing how to switch off at the end of the day can lead to a more productive day in the long term. And if our homes are where we go to relax, it is sensible to make them as tranquil as possible, especially if you spend time at home during the day.

Our daily lives and the world around us may seem full of sources of stress, yet with planning, thought and a positive outlook we can make every aspect and every situation a source of peace, pleasure and tranquillity.

Try not to be a slave to a schedule – take the opportunity to slow down and enjoy the many things each day has to offer.

Change your lifestyle and do 10 minutes of stretching, yoga or Pilates each morning – it will improve your health and fitness and give you more energy for the coming day.

Diet

'You are what you eat' is one of those irritating platitudes that happens to be true. Stuff yourself with junk food or drink too much alcohol and you will feel tired, bloated and sluggish. Eat a well-balanced diet with plenty of fresh fruit and vegetables and you will feel much more alert and full of increased vitality and vigour.

A balanced diet

Eating the right balance of food can make a big difference to your health and vitality. Your body needs a diet that consists of about 50% carbohydrates, 30% fat, 15% protein and plenty of fibre, vitamins and minerals and water.

Carbohydrates

These provide the body's basic source of energy. Simple carbohydrates, such as sugars, give instant energy but have no nutritional value. Complex carbohydrates, found in bread, pasta, rice, potatoes, cereals and pulses, are better for you because they

The foods that contain complex carbohydrates also contain fibre, minerals and essential vitamins.

Fats

These are essential for growth and healthy digestion, but too much fat can make you overweight and cause serious health problems.

Foods containing high amounts of fat and protein, such as milk, cheese, chocolate and bacon, are best eaten in small quantities.

Protein

The body needs a daily supply of protein for cell growth, maintenance and repair. Most Westerners get much more protein than they need, which usually becomes converted into fat.

Pulses, rice and nuts are high in fibre, carbohydrate and protein, and provide essential bulk for the diet.

Fibre

Dietary fibre, found in nuts, pulses, rice, cereals and wholegrains, prevents constipation, lowers blood cholesterol and helps protect against bowel disorders and diseases.

Vitamins and minerals

Although only needed in small amounts, these are essential for maintaining good health.

Foods for relaxation

Foods that contain calcium, magnesium and vitamin B6 are known to have a tranquilizing effect. Green leafy vegetables, milk and dairy products, apricots, bananas, nuts and yeast extract are just some of the foods that will help you feel calmer. Meat, milk and eggs contain tryptophan, an essential amino acid that turns into the important brain chemical serotonin, which enhances mood and regulates sleep.

What to eat

The healthiest diet is one that is high in fruit, vegetables, grains and pulses and low in animal and dairy products. Nutritional guidelines are based on the traditional eating habits of people who live around the Mediterranean, where there is a history of long life expectancy and low rates of heart disease.

- Complex carbohydrates should form half your daily diet.
- Eat at least five portions of fruit and vegetables a day, preferably organic.
- Try to consume low-fat dairy foods.
- Eat oily fish at least once a week.
- Limit your consumption of red meat and cheeses.
- Eat plenty of fibre-rich foods.
- Reduce your salt intake – use in cooking only.
- Limit your sugar intake – try not to use too much in tea and coffee.
- Eat fresh foods whenever possible and cut back on processed foods.
- Drink alcohol in moderation, and try to have at least two alcohol-free days a week.
- Drink enough fluids to keep your urine pale – at least two litres of water a day to flush out toxins. A glass of water every couple of hours will make you feel much more alert.
- Limit your consumption of tea, coffee, cola-type drinks and chocolate.

When to eat

Optimum nutrition means eating the right foods at the right time, and good health depends on eating regular meals. Breakfast kick-starts the metabolism and boosts blood-sugar levels: if you miss it you may feel tired and unable to concentrate. Lunch should be the biggest meal of the day because this is when the metabolism is at its most effective. Have a light supper at least two hours before you go to bed as it is hard for the body to digest a large meal at the end of the day.

How to eat

A leisurely meal is much more enjoyable than a snack on the hoof, and infinitely more relaxing. The next time you eat, sit down and savour each mouthful. Experience the different flavours and notice how they complement each other. If you are drinking a glass of wine, wait before swallowing and allow the complexities of taste to become apparent. As you chew, appreciate the different textures of food. If you take time to appreciate food you are less likely to overeat and more likely to chew properly, which will benefit your digestion.

The problem with stimulants

Stimulants, such as tea, coffee, chocolate and sugar, are chemicals that act on the body like rocket fuel, giving a quick burst of energy followed by a rapid burnout. They boost your energy levels by stimulating the adrenal glands, which sit on top of the kidneys and release hormones that give your body's cells an express delivery of glucose. You soon become caught in a vicious circle whereby you need more of the stimulant to get the same effect until you become dependent upon it. Stimulants also contain toxins, and your body has only a finite capacity to deal with these. As your body's chemistry becomes more exhausted, your body is in a constant state of red alert and you become prey to anxiety, fatigue, and mood swings.

After eight o'clock at night you should have no more than a light meal to ensure effective digestion.

Reducing dependencies on stimulants, such as coffee, tea, chocolate and sugar will make you feel much calmer and healthier.

Reducing stimulant dependence

Cutting down on stimulants is essential to helping you feel relaxed. Keep a diary for three days to identify which stimulants you rely on and be honest about just how much of each you are consuming. Try to identify at which point in the day you usually take them (as a reaction to a stressful situation, or as a pick-me-up, for example) and see if a pattern emerges. Try to replace these behaviour patterns with healthier ones, such as eating a piece of fruit instead of a bar of chocolate.

Cutting out stimulants completely is impossible for most people, but the way to cut down is to target one at a time and reduce your intake until it is no longer a daily necessity. You will probably feel groggy and get regular headaches for the first few days (particularly if you are addicted to coffee), but persevere and you will soon feel much better and healthier.

Nicotine and alcohol dependence are very hard habits to overcome, and may require professional counselling or group therapy.

Bowl of fruit

Buy a large fruit bowl and keep it well stocked with plenty of fresh, appetising fruit, such as bananas, apples and oranges. Next time you want a snack, avoid the biscuit tin and head for the fruit bowl instead.

The importance of exercise

One of the first things we neglect to do when stressed is to exercise. However, research has proven that exercise is a tremendous relaxation aid. Regular exercise frees your mind and your body: it can improve mood, increase self-esteem, reduce anxiety, promote sleep, reduce high blood pressure, and help weight loss.

How exercise helps you relax

1. Exercise stimulates the appetite. Those who exercise regularly tend to eat better, and good nutrition helps your body to manage stress more effectively.
2. Exercise causes the release of the body's natural painkillers, endorphins, which reduce anxiety and leave you feeling relaxed and in a better mood.
3. Exercise releases adrenaline, which builds up in your body when you are stressed.
4. Muscular movement enables the body's systems to work more efficiently, removing toxins.
5. Physical activity makes you feel more confident about your body.
6. Exercise forces you to make time for yourself, distracting you from daily pressures, which will in turn reduce stress. Repetitive exercise such as walking, running or swimming is a golden opportunity for reflection, meditation and mental relaxation.
7. Regular exercise will make you tired and help you sleep better (although strenuous exercise just before bedtime can stimulate the body too much).
8. Exercise promotes deep breathing, which is key to relaxation. And deep breathing will supply more oxygen to the brain, which improves mental stamina.

Practising yoga is a great way of improving your physical health and reducing stress into the bargain.

Getting started

It is important to choose an activity you enjoy, because you are then much more likely to stick to it. Find an activity that suits your personality, and think of exercise as a joy and a means of relaxation rather than a chore. If you can keep to a regular programme for at least six months, the chances are that you will continue for much longer. Consider your physical limitations and don't push your body too severely. Build up gradually, especially if you have not exercised for a while.

Improving general fitness

You don't have to give a lot of time, or join a gym or spend lots of money to become fit. As little as 10 minutes a day of walking, dancing, gardening, swimming or cycling can make a significant difference to your overall fitness levels, dramatically reduce stress and make you feel more energetic, healthier and happier.

You can choose forms of exercise that are easily incorporated into your daily life: walk or cycle to work if you can; walk up the stairs instead of taking the lift; get off the bus to work one or two stops earlier and walk the remaining distance; regularly take the dog for a walk; take the children to the park at the weekend; or just put on some music and dance around the kitchen.

Caution

Consult a doctor before embarking on a vigorous programme of exercise if your lifestyle is very sedentary, if you are pregnant, if you are over 45 years of age, if you have a history of high blood pressure, high cholesterol levels, heart or lung disease, or if you are a heavy smoker or considerably overweight.

Cycling is a great way to get plenty of fresh air and improve your cardiovascular fitness.

World of work

Most of us spend the majority of our day at work, and research shows that the hours we spend working are constantly increasing. You are unlikely to be able to change either the prevailing work ethic or your working environment, but you can keep hold of your priorities and devise strict routines to ensure you make the most of your time.

How to organise your day

If you're one of those people who, having rushed out of the door in the morning, has to return because you have forgotten something, or if you are someone who spends much of your working day flapping about until you reach home in a state of exhaustion, you need to get organised and regain control.

Try out the following advice to take control of your day and reduce stress:

- Prepare as much as possible the night before – put your clothes out, or lay the breakfast table, for example.
- Get up at least 10 minutes earlier than usual to give yourself the extra time to complete whatever it is that causes you to rush.
- Do not switch on the television as this will distract you and make you late.
- Do not answer the phone unless you think it could be really important.
- Just before leaving the house, go over your mental checklist to reassure yourself you have everything you need.

Making a checklist is an effective way of organising a busy day – you could even pin it to the refrigerator to make sure you haven't forgotten anything.

At work

Having a work routine helps you define your achievements and leave the stresses of work behind at the end of the day. Once a week, plan a weekly schedule. Then spend the first 15 minutes of each working day thinking about what you wish to achieve. It helps to make a list, but don't make it too long as this can be daunting and demotivating.

- Don't try to do too many things at once.
- Prioritise, and do the essential things first.
- Try to tackle at least one thing on your list that you really do not like doing – you will have a great sense of achievement when this task is completed.
- Leave half an hour a day for the unexpected.
- Delegate as many tasks as possible – don't take on everything yourself.
- If you can't delegate, ask for help.
- Learn to say 'no' politely, without feeling the need to justify yourself.
- Get a good diary and use it.
- Meetings should be to the point – always make it clear when it will end.
- If you are delayed, phone and inform the person you are meeting; if you have to break an appointment, try to give as much notice as possible.
- Take time at the end of the day to review what you've done and to congratulate yourself on your achievements.

Telephone taming

- If you have to make a number of phone calls, group them together – it is much more efficient.
- Use an answering machine and switch off your mobile phone if you do not wish to be disturbed.
- If you work from home, invest in an extra line and don't answer the business one out of office hours.
- Do not answer the phone just before or during meals – if it is really important, the person will phone back.

Don't let the telephone take over your life – only answer calls when it suits you, and only make calls when you have plenty of time.

Work space

A cluttered desk makes it more difficult to work effectively. Tidy your desk at the end of each day. Make use of in, out and pending trays, and keep everything you need close to hand. Keep a supply of stationery and pens within easy reach of your desk, and dispose of those that no longer work.

Pause for thought

Most of us are governed by clocks, constantly under one deadline or another in order to become more efficient and productive. As slaves of time, we constantly rush to get things done, frequently making mistakes, instead of thinking about what we are trying to achieve. Taking a moment to stop and think gives you the opportunity to act with greater consciousness and react more appropriately to the situation. A pause also lets you say 'no' and avoid committing yourself to too many things at once.

Take a break

It is universally recognised that to work for long hours without a regular break is damaging for your health and can on occasion be extremely dangerous. It's just like driving – you have to stop every couple of hours as your concentration and abilities begin to fail. Many office chairs are bad for the posture, and long hours spent staring at a computer screen can cause eyestrain, neck ache and backache. Get up, stretch, and walk around at least once an hour. Take time off for lunch and eat away from your desk if possible. Remember that by law you are entitled to have regular breaks, and you will be much more productive if you take them.

At work, take time to enjoy a tasty, nutritious snack and recharge your batteries.

When to switch off

Don't fall into the trap of thinking that the longer you spend at work, the more you will get done when in fact the opposite is more likely. Working excessively long hours and taking work home is counterproductive. Keeping work and home separate, and being able to spend quality time with your family, is essential – if you spend your leisure time relaxing, you will return to work refreshed and be able to give it your full attention.

Instant calm at work

If you are being thrown into a state of panic by an approaching deadline, make a conscious effort to calm down. Instruct yourself to stop, then close your eyes and breathe slowly and deeply. Feel yourself becoming more relaxed; notice your heartbeat slowing down. Alternatively, follow the steps for quick and easy meditation on page 25.

Time off: holidays

A holiday is a chance to rest and recharge your batteries, but all too often it turns into another stressful event. Mental and physical preparation will make potential difficulties easier to deal with. Planning is key to a successful holiday. First of all, choose a holiday that suits you and your family. Find out as much as you can about your destination before you go so that you know what your itinerary will be, and what to pack. A few days before, prepare yourself mentally by making an effort to relax and slow down – maybe take an extra day off work to unwind further.

Relaxing at home

Your home is your sanctuary. Your living environment has a tremendous impact on your sense of well-being. An untidy, cluttered home painted in dingy colours makes you feel stressed, while a bright, tidy home that reflects your character and family will create a happy, positive and loving atmosphere where you can truly relax.

Light and space

Natural light is best for your eyes, so make the most of daylight and position desks near windows. A spacious, airy and light environment is the most relaxing, but you can create space by keeping surfaces clear.

Turn down the volume

Noise can be incredibly stressful, even though you may not be aware of it. Only watch television if there's a programme you really want to see, and turn it off at mealtimes. Soothe your soul by listening to music instead.

To create a serene atmosphere in your home, avoid harsh fluorescent lighting, and use soft light or candles in the evening.

Ten top tips for a tidy home

1. Remove your shoes at the door – it stops you bringing dirt into the house.
2. Do your least favourite household chore first.
3. Keep a waste-paper bin in each room.
4. The less you have, the easier it is to keep clean. Clear away clutter once a month and have a good sort out once a year. If you haven't used something in the last year, then you probably don't need it.
5. Keep work surfaces tidy.
6. Storage space is essential – invest in extra cupboards if you need them.
7. Encourage your children to tidy up after themselves.
8. To discourage random clutter, keep a 'lost property box' in the living room.
9. Tidy up after a meal rather than leaving the dishes until morning.
10. Organise a rota so that each family member plays their part.

Feng shui

Feng shui is the ancient Chinese art of arranging living and working spaces so that they are in harmony with the flow of *qi*, the universal life force (see page 19). Landscapes, buildings and rooms are said to have their own flow of *qi*, and feng shui encourages blocked or diminished *qi* to move more freely in a certain area by altering its layout. A feng shui practitioner will make a detailed assessment of each room in your house and suggest changes, such as a new colour scheme or repositioning of plants and furniture.

To improve the feng shui in your home, clear up clutter and make sure there is plenty of space around furniture.

Encourage your children to help keep the house clean and tidy.

The world around you

Those who appreciate nature are generally happier, calmer people. Today, many people live in noisy, polluted, overcrowded cities where concrete predominates over greenery. But you don't have to live in the country to benefit from nature. Take a walk through the park or simply sit in the garden to relax and truly appreciate your surroundings.

The great outdoors

Ultimately, a relaxed state of being depends on you spending plenty of time outdoors. Light is recognised as essential for regulating the body's internal clock, which controls hormone production and sleep. Spend holidays in the mountains or at the seaside to get maximum benefit from light and fresh air.

Plants pour oxygen into the environment while soaking up carbon dioxide and other toxins.

Park life

A walk in the park will help you to reconnect with the natural world. Visit the same park during each of the seasons so that you can appreciate nature's life cycle. Take time to notice the colours of the trees and flowers and the different smells. Breathe in deeply and inhale large amounts of fresh air.

Gardening

Gardening is a wonderfully relaxing activity because it releases physical tension, thus reducing the amount of circulating stress hormones in the body, while the act of cultivation in itself is soothing for the soul. Novice gardeners can nurture hardy, low-maintenance plants (see gardening books for inspiration and practical advice). If you don't have a garden, plant a window box instead.

Improve the oxygen levels in your home by keeping some pot plants.

Never judge a day by the weather

All too often we let the weather determine our mood: on a sunny day, a good mood; on a rainy day, gloom and introspection. Think positively about the different aspects of weather instead: the cool, crispness of snow, the rain that nurtures crops or the fact that thunderstorms do literally clear the air.

A sense of time

Your body adheres to a natural sense of time without you even being aware of it. Ask yourself how often you really need to know what the time is.

Seasons

Air conditioning and modern central heating systems have removed much of the impact of the changing seasons, but if you can live in harmony with nature's cycle you will appreciate life much more. Spring, traditionally the season of hope and renewal, is the time for starting afresh, clearing your life of clutter and setting change in motion. Summer, associated with happiness and light, brings a sense of freedom and carefreeness. Autumn, the season of fruition and abundance, is the time for reflecting upon what you have achieved and counting the year's blessings. Winter is a time of rest, retreat and reflection on what has passed.

When you come home from work, and at weekends, take off your watch and remove yourself from time pressures.

Getting a good night's sleep

A good night's sleep is a period of profound rest that is essential for your physical and emotional well-being. Time spent sleeping is often the best way to recover from illness or cope with stress. When sleeping, your body will repair and regenerate itself, and your can mind resolve outstanding problems through dreams.

What is sleep?

Sleep is a naturally occurring state of unconsciousness, when the electrical activity of the brain is more rhythmical than when awake and reacts less to outside stimuli. There are two basic sleep states: deep sleep, known as non-REM (NREM) sleep, when the body repairs itself, interrupted by episodes of Rapid Eye Movement (REM) sleep, when most dreaming takes place.

Establishing a calming routine that helps you wind down and relax before bedtime will go a long way in helping you to get a good night's sleep.

How much sleep?

The amount of sleep necessary to be fully rested varies for each individual, and it decreases with age. Most adults get by on seven to eight hours sleep, though some sleep experts claim we need more. The elderly can function on five or six hours a night.

Sleep problems

Sleep is one of the first things to suffer when you are stressed, and too little sleep will make you tired and irritable. A lack of sleep is itself a stress factor, and it is all too easy to become locked into a cycle of sleeplessness that is difficult to break. There are many different kinds of sleeplessness, including not being able to go to sleep, frequent waking, and waking too early in the morning.

Sleep enhancers

- Don't go to bed hungry, but avoid large meals before bedtime.
- Bananas, milky drinks and wholemeal biscuits are calming foods and ideal for eating before you go to sleep.
- Caffeine, alcohol and nicotine all disturb sleep. Drink a cup of warm herbal tea before bedtime – chamomile is particularly effective.
- Exercise during the day will remove stress hormones from your body but avoid any form of exercise (apart from sex) at least three hours before bedtime.

Drink something calming and tasty before you sleep.

Establishing a routine

- Stop work at least an hour before bedtime to calm mental activity.
- A warm bath before bedtime will relax your muscles and soothe your body.
- Go to bed at the same time each night and get up at a regular time.
- Your bedroom needs to be a place for sleeping rather than an extension of you office or living room – keep it quiet and warm.
- If you really cannot sleep, get up and go into another room and read a book or watch something light on television until you feel sleepy.

The importance of dreams

We all have dreams, although we may not remember them when we wake up. Dreaming is thought to act as a psychological safety valve, allowing us to work through problems, emotions and anxieties so we can start afresh each day.

Natural remedies for relaxation

Natural remedies are very effective in reducing the effects of stress and restoring the balance of body and mind. They are an enjoyable way of improving well-being and have been used around the world for thousands of years.

Aromatherapy

Essential oils distilled from plants, flowers and resins can be used to promote good health and help you relax. Your sense of smell is directly linked to memories and mood (see page 29). Among other things, essential oils can be antidepressant, relieve pain and tension, ease headaches, act as a tonic, and help to ensure a good night's sleep.

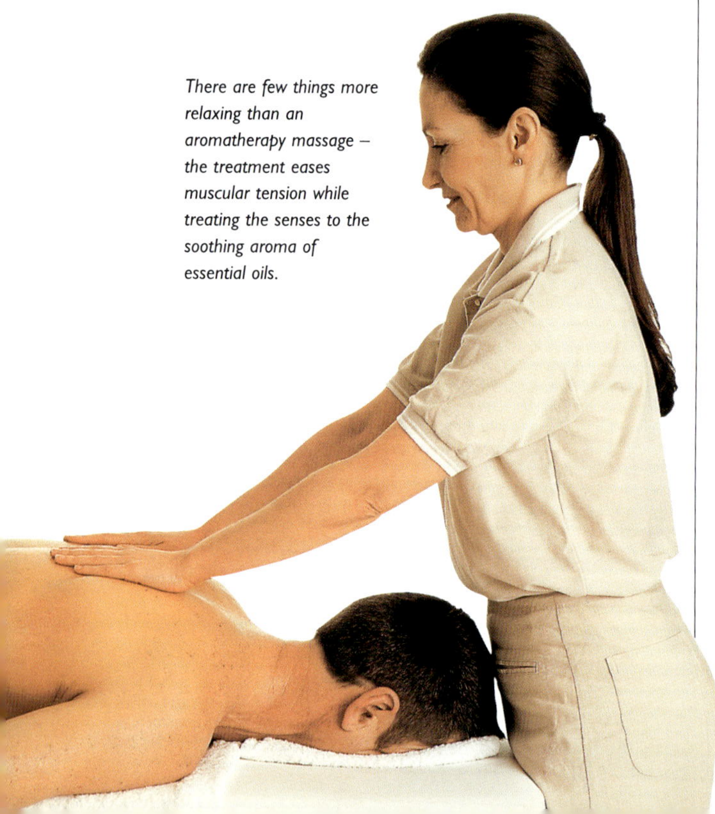

There are few things more relaxing than an aromatherapy massage – the treatment eases muscular tension while treating the senses to the soothing aroma of essential oils.

Oils can be inhaled, used in compresses to relieve pain, added to bathwater or massage oil, or used in a vaporiser.

Massage

An aromatherapy massage combines the relaxing properties of various oils with the benefits of touch. Dilute a few drops of two or three essential oils in a carrier oil such as sweet almond or apricot kernel oil; add a little jojoba oil for very dry skins. Blend six drops of essential oil with 4 tsp (15–20ml) of carrier oil to make enough for a full body massage.

Baths

Only add neat oils to bathwater if they are guaranteed to be non-irritants, such as Roman chamomile and lavender; otherwise, dilute in a carrier oil. Add five drops then swirl the bathwater around to disperse the oils before stepping into the bath. Oils added to bathwater are inhaled and partly absorbed by the skin, bringing immediate physical benefits.

Ten relaxing essential oils

Bergamot (*Citrus bergamia*): soothing, uplifting and good for tension and depression.

Chamomile (*Chamaemelum nobile*): calming; suitable for insomnia.

Jasmine (*Jasminum officinale*): a stimulant or a sedative, according to need; excellent antidepressant and aphrodisiac.

Juniper (*Juniperus communis*): good for fatigue and boosting self-esteem.

Lavender (*Lavandula angustifolia*): a very useful and popular oil, used for relaxing and as an antidepressant and painkiller.

Lemon balm (*Melissa officinalis*): long used to banish melancholy; balances the emotions.

Rosemary (*Rosmarinus officinalis*): refreshing and stimulating.

Sandalwood (*Santalum album*): used as an antidepressant and aphrodisiac.

Vetiver (*Vetiveria zizanioides*): balances the nervous system; good for insomnia.

Ylang ylang (*Cananga odorata*): calming; used as an aphrodisiac and good for panic attacks.

Cautions

- Always dilute oils before use (although lavender and tea tree can be used neat in first aid situations).
- Some oils are not safe to use in pregnancy.
- Seek professional advice before using essential oils if you have a long-standing medical condition such as heart disease, diabetes or high blood pressure.
- Many oils are not suitable for small children, so check first.
- Some oils react adversely to sunlight.
- Do not use steam inhalations if you have a breathing disorder such as asthma.
- Never take oils internally, unless professionally prescribed.

Vaporisation

Filling a room with an aroma of your choice is the easiest way to enjoy essential oils. Add a few drops to a saucer of water and place on a radiator, or place in a burner.

Certain oils can improve mood and concentration, and are deeply relaxing.

Herbalism

Herbal remedies use plants to restore health and strengthen the body, enabling it to recover more easily. Many synthetic drugs, such as aspirin, are derived from plants, but herbalism uses the whole plant, believing that the complex mix of components creates a herbal 'synergy' that is more effective than isolated constituents.

Using herbal remedies

Herbs are usually taken in the form of infusions, tinctures and decoctions. They can also be made into ointments, massage oils and creams to rub into the skin, and added to hot or cold compresses. Many preparations can be bought ready-made from health stores.

Decoctions

Tough plant material such as roots and bark are boiled in water to extract the active ingredients. The liquid is then strained and taken hot or cold. Boil down the liquid and add sugar to make a syrup.

Herbal remedies are a natural way of easing away the stresses of modern living. Remember not to exceed the recommended dose.

Infusions

An infusion is a herbal tea. Herbs are placed in a teapot, covered with boiling water and left to steam for about 10 minutes. The liquid is drained into a cup and drunk hot or cold. It can be kept in the refrigerator for 24 hours and can be reheated.

Tinctures

Tinctures are made by steeping herbs in a mixture of alcohol and water. The alcohol acts as a preservative (the mixture can be kept for up to two years) and also extracts the medicinal constituents of the plant.

Caution

- Seek professional advice before taking herbal medicine if you are pregnant, or if you have a long-standing medical condition such as heart disease, diabetes or high blood pressure.
- Consult a qualified herbalist before using herbal remedies if you are taking prescribed medication.

Popular herbs for relaxation

Chamomile (*Chamaemelum nobile*): promotes feelings of relaxation and settles digestion.

Echinacea (*Echinacea purpurea*): strengthens the immune system.

Ginkgo (*Ginkgo biloba*): improves blood flow and the activity of neurotransmitters in the brain; beneficial for sufferers of tinnitus.

Lavender (*Lavandula angustifolia*): lifts mood and relieves indigestion and headaches.

Lime flower (*Tilia cordata*): effective relaxant that reduces anxiety and restlessness.

St John's wort (*Hypericum perforatum*): a well-known antidepressant without side-effects.

Skullcap (*Scutellaria lateriflora*): a calming nerve tonic that reduces anxiety and restlessness.

Vervain (*Verbena officinalis*): sedative nerve tonic good for insomnia and for relieving tension and depression.

Flower remedies

Flower essences, made by infusing flower heads in water then preserving the strained water in brandy, were developed in the 1920s by an English doctor and homeopath, Edward Bach. He believed that flowers possessed healing properties that could treat emotional illnesses. He thought that harmful emotions were the main cause of disease and identified seven states of mind – fear, uncertainty, lack of interest in present circumstances, loneliness, over-sensitivity, despondency and over-concern for the welfare of others – which he subdivided into 38 negative feelings, each associated with a particular plant. Bach flower remedies aim to restore the harmony of mind and body necessary for good health. That flower remedies work is indisputable, although no one knows how: they do not work in any biochemical way, but therapists believe the remedies contain the energy, or imprint, of the plant and provide a stimulus to kick-start your own healing mechanism.

Glossary

Adrenaline
This is the hormone secreted by the adrenal glands that prepares the body for 'fight or flight' and has widespread effects on circulation, the muscles and the metabolic rate.

Amino acids
These are organic compounds found in proteins. Essential amino acids cannot be made by the body and must be obtained from food.

Autonomic nervous system
The part of the nervous system responsible for automatic body functions, such as breathing, perspiration, salivation, digestion and heart rate. The sympathetic division activates the body's alarm response and prepares for action; the parasympathetic division is concerned with restoring and conserving bodily resources.

Cardiovascular system
The heart and blood vessels.

Central nervous system
The vast network of cells that carry information in the form of electrical impulses to and from all parts of the body to cause bodily activity.

Cholesterol
A fat-like substance present in the blood and most tissues; high levels can damage blood vessel walls and lead to a thickening of the arteries. Excessively high levels of cholesterol can lead to heart problems.

Endorphin
A painkiller produced by the body.

Hormone
A substance produced in one part of the body that travels in the bloodstream to another organ or tissue, where it acts to modify structure or functions.

Hyperventilation
This is breathing at an abnormally rapid rate, which can lead to loss of consciousness as blood acidity falls dramatically.

Immune system
These are the organs responsible for immunity with the ability to resist infection.

Metabolism
Chemical processes that take place in the body, which enable continued growth and functioning of the whole system.

Neurotransmitter
A chemical that is released from nerve endings to transmit impulses between nerves, muscles and glands.

Proteins
Essential constituents of the body that form its structural material and, as enzymes and hormones, regulate body functions.

Qi
The universal 'life force' of traditional Chinese medicine (also known as *chi*); similar to *prana* in Ayurvedic medicine.

Serotonin
A neurotransmitter whose levels in the brain have an important effect on mood.

Stimulant
Something that has an uplifting effect on the mind or body. Well-known stimulants include nicotine, alcohol, sugar, coffee, tea and chocolate.

Useful addresses

Autogenic Training

British Association for Autogenic
Training and Therapy
c/o The Royal London Homeopathic
Hospital NHS Trust
Great Ormond Street
London WC1N 3HR

Alexander Technique

The Society of Teachers of the Alexander Technique
20 London House
266 Fulham Road
London SW10 9EL

Aromatherapy

Aromatherapy Organisations Council
3 Latymer Close
Braybooke
Market Harborough
Leics LE16 8LN

Herbalism

National Institute of Medical Herbalists
56 Longbrook Street
Exeter
Devon EX4 6AG

Hypnotherapy

The Central Register of Advanced Hypnotherapists
28 Finsbury Park Road
London N4 2JX

Massage

British Massage Therapy Council
Greenbank House
65a Adelphi Street
Preston
Lancs PR1 7BH

Meditation
School of Meditation
158 Holland Park Road
London W11 4UH

Nutrition
The Institute for Optimum Nutrition
Blades Court
Deodar Road
London SW15 2NU

Reflexology
British Reflexology Association
Monks Orchard
Whitbourne
Worcester WR6 5RB

Relaxation and Breathing
The Relaxation for Living Trust
Foxhills
30 Victoria Avenue
Shanklin
Isle of Wight PO37 6LS

T'ai Chi
T'ai Chi Union for Great Britain
23 Oakwood Avenue
Mitcham
Surrey CR4 3DQ

Yoga
British Wheel of Yoga
1 Hamilton Place
Sleaford
Notts NG34 7ES

Visualisation
United Kingdom Council for Psychotherapy
167–69 Great Portland Street
London W1N 5FB

Index

YOUNG WRITERS

I Have a Dream

The Future Speaks

EQUALITY TOGETHER RESPECT DREAM INCLUSIVE STRENGTH COURAGE PROTECT SHAPE BRAVE FREEDOM HEALING KIND GROW HOPE PEACE STRIVE KINDNESS PASSION CHANGE CARE SHINE AMBITION CREATE RISE IMAGINE PROTECT EXPLORE

First published in Great Britain in 2025 by:

Young Writers
Remus House
Coltsfoot Drive
Peterborough
PE2 9BF
Telephone: 01733 890066
Website: www.youngwriters.co.uk

Book Design by Ashley Janson

Softback ISBN 978-1-80699-020-7
Printed and bound in the UK by BookPrintingUK
Website: www.bookprintinguk.com
YB0662I

FOREWORD

Our latest competition I Have A Dream asked young writers to reach for something beyond the ordinary: to articulate their hopes, their longings, or their creativity. Whether for themselves, their community, or the wider world, whether grounded reality or exploring imagination, these poems showcase dreams in all their forms.

At this age, writing becomes more than expression, it becomes a space for self-discovery. To question, to rebel, to reflect. This competition also gave these young adults the opportunity to focus on the positives, to consider change for the better, and to just have fun with words.

At Young Writers, we believe in the importance of visibility. When young people see their words in print, it gives them pride in themselves, confidence in their own ability and hopefully a spark to keep on creating. It shows them that their ideas matter, their stories matter. Poetry here is a bridge between inner life and shared worlds: creative, imaginative, but rooted in truth.

Within these pages you'll find a chorus of voices – some fierce, some gentle, some rebellious, some hopeful, some fun – each one sharing a vision. May these dreams move you, challenge you, inspire you to imagine boldly, to write bravely, and to never stop dreaming.

We encourage young writers to express themselves and address subjects that matter to them, which sometimes means writing about sensitive or contentious topics. If you have been affected by any issues raised in this book, details on where to find help can be found at **www.youngwriters.co.uk/contact-lines**

CONTENTS

THE Poems

You Must Be The Change

I'm Aneel and I am twelve,
I'm a Year Eight student and into the future I will delve.
Dancing is a passion, it makes me feel alive,
I always work hard; it's for perfection I always strive.
Following the rules is something I always do,
Even if I'm struggling, I always get through!
When I am older, a lawyer I will be,
I'll work hard in my exams, just you wait and see.
Our world is important, we must look after the land,
Chopping down our trees should definitely be banned!
My dream for the world is for it to be plastic-free,
Let's all work together and jump around with glee.
I have a dream that my family's lives are filled with peace,
We'll work together piece by piece.
My friends are reliable, funny and kind,
Friends like these are a very rare find.
Travelling the world is a very big dream,
I'll do it with my friends—we'll travel as a team!
We'll sightsee, and eat, and dance galore,
I really cannot wait to travel and explore!
I'll change the world one bit at a time,
I'm just getting started, I'm still in my prime!
All our dreams can come true if we have the courage to pursue them enough,
Nothing is impossible—there's no such word as tough!

Aneel Kaur Kooner (12)

Dreams Impossible

I live in my head mostly.
In mangled dreams and what could've been.
What should've been
What can't be.
I live in my head mostly,
Where this cruel world is simply fiction
And remains enmeshed into the books of my imagination,
Eternally trapped in the ebony webs of their words,
But even when I open my eyes, they're still relentlessly cruel.
I live in my heart too sometimes,
But I don't like it there.
The pretty paintings on the white walls wilt at every turn,
And the red cement on the broken pipes starts to melt and pool around my ankles
When I turn on the tap.
All the grins frozen fresh in the photo frames atop the shelves are melting,
The anatomy of happiness is decaying before my eyes,
And deep within me.
Eyes are lifeless and I see the corpse of memory everywhere.
I walk upon dilapidated pillars and I build upon nothingness.
When I distract myself from this nightmare with picture books and diaries from the past,
I am confronted by the spectre of your love,

Tell me, why do you torment me so?
I dust your absence off of my kitchen cabinets
And I frame it on my bedside table.
This house is strewn with your presence,
And yet I don't see you.
Bricks are always falling out of the severed ceiling,
And the squalid floorboards are rotting beneath my feet.
The choking hearth of the fireplace has collected heaps of ash,
But I cannot rekindle even a spark to begin to thaw the frigidity of these four walls.
I live in my heart too sometimes,

But it floods a lot and I am always on the cusp of drowning.
So I drill three holes in my heart so that the water can tear out
And my lungs can die instead.
But I've never lived in my soul.
I've always thought it was boring. Ancient. Irrelevant.
See, before, when my soul used to invite me over,
I used to make excuses not to come and claimed that I was struggling to contain the contents of my head.
I used to say that my heart was flooding again and that I needed to reopen its holes.
I told my soul to wait for my visit for just a few more days,
That I would be there as quickly as I could,
And I told my lover to scatter flowers around my soul in order to brighten up its dull complexion.

I told my lover to wash the dishes in my heart for me,
For my own hands were being wrung by far more pressing responsibilities.
I told my lover to tend to my soul in my absence,
To clothe her shuddering figure with his love,
To then strangle her with his cologne,
For I knew that he was the only one who could.
I continued to make excuses as to why I couldn't just visit,
Until one day my soul stopped inviting me over,
And my lover stopped calling too.
Nobody walked behind me, not beside me, nor even in front of me.
This newfound vulnerability was daunting.
It made my heart stop beating.
It fractured my mind, so that all the demons would be untethered!
I was utterly dejected, without the comfort of attention.
I'd found solace in being wanted, cherished it in the gaps between my fingers
Where it was always slipping to, and clutched it so closely to my lacerations,
Because the way it fondled my heart was foreign to my memories,
But familiar when it was draped across my shoulders like a pleasant weight.
Alas, I had forgotten I wasn't needed;
After this revelation, I don't know which of the fragments of my being have left to dream in a utopian realm,
Nor do I have any idea of which of those loyal blades remained true to me.

I have indulged in these highs for too long,
Settled in the cold warmth of the dope too comfortably,
And forsaken how my feet are still entrenched in the dirt of the lows,
Whilst I was engrossed in my head and my heart.
I ventured over to the doorstep of my soul one day,
And saw dying ivy inching up the door.
I crept, to the barely breathing windows,
And saw that they were smashed.
I peered inside my soul apprehensively,
And all I could see was darkness.
I tried to climb in through the window, but a jagged edge of the shattered window caught on my leg and drew blood.
Out of anger, I shattered the remaining windows and looked inside the house,
My fury heightening at the filthiness of it all.
And then I ventured back to the doorstep of my soul,
And noticed for the first time the white doorknob.
I rapped on the door with my knuckles,
And when no one answered, I twisted the doorknob but it didn't budge.
When I withdrew my clenched fists, seething with anger and cursing my soul for not letting me in,
I saw the white doorknob fade.
At first, I didn't know if it was my head messing with me.
Or the beating of my heart that was obscuring my vision.
But then I saw the white doorknob turn black like the rest of the house,

And I knew my soul wouldn't let me back in,
Because I cannot take my heart out of its state of disrepair
And live in my head too often,
In mangled dreams amidst lunging flames of self-pity,
And remain immersed in my unhealthy obsessions with what could've been,
What should've been,
What can't be.
I cannot just destroy my soul, too.
Alas, this sentiment is a dream impossible.

Noor Mahroof (16)

The World Awaits

I wish to discover what was hidden in the past,
To clamber up mountains and gaze upon the patchwork green,
To go from country to culture until I'm a friend of the last,
To fill up my memory with all that I've seen.
I wish to lie under the stars in an unfamiliar sky,
To survey the clouds from an unfamiliar view,
To taste the flavours on the wind as they blow by,
To observe the landscape change as I progress through.
I wish to be unknowing of the streets,
To ask for directions around every corner I take,
To savour the delectable, foreign treats,
To share stories with newly discovered friends I make.
I wish to walk along golden sands,
To hear cerulean waves thundering towards me,
To hear the distant hum of seaside bands,
To listen to tales of creatures lurking beneath the sea.
I wish to draw in the scent of damp pine,
To overhear the chatter of the concealed birds,
To glance up and see ivy and branches entwine,
To hear the cracks of twigs from deer in herds.
I wish to traverse the land as I see fit,
To set sail across oceans to reach lands far away,
To take to the skies on planes and soar, bit by bit,
To travel the world, I will experience it someday.

Sophie Neal (13)

It Must Be More Than A Dream

Like a girl
She's a girl
Not a girl
Bad girl
Good girl
Girls
Pink, makeup, dolls
And for boys—cars, trees, dragons, trolls
And why?

In my dream
Men and women are equal
I didn't say the same
We're created differently, not the same
Those who treat us the same
Treat both unfairly
In my dream
We're treated equally
Equality
Doesn't mean everyone wears a uniform colour or uniform dress
Doesn't mean one form to conform to is the best
Doesn't mean that everyone has the same job, same home, same life
Equality just means that we're treated right.

In my mind, equality means accommodating for everyone's needs
There's no way
To remove all the planet's problems instantly
No way
To prevent the harm of some
Equality doesn't mean that in one's death all must die
It doesn't mean that because of some lies
The whole world must be consumed by untruth
It doesn't mean that one person's honesty can remove prejudice altogether
Equality
Means I need to be treated fairly
Equality
Means I've never cared for dolls
Always found Barbies boring
Trees to climb felt like home
But equality doesn't mean that women aren't allowed to dream of a home
Equality only means that they shouldn't be forced to do so
Equality doesn't mean it's wrong for women to cook
But it's wrong for every recipe, every cookbook
To be used by women more than by men.

It isn't wrong for little boys to love nature and cars
It isn't wrong for them to reach for the stars
But it's correct that a little girl should reach her maximum capacity just the same.

Equality—that's my dream
I suppose it's a dream we all dream and we all have
Somewhere in our hearts
But when conflict starts
When someone doesn't agree
We run
We hide
In no one do we confide
And that's not right.

A dream we all dream, we all know
Is a dream that should get deeper, should expand
Should take on new meaning
Should know
We should know
At least what it is by now that we're striving for
What do we want at our core?
And that's equality
For me
That's equality.

My dream is developed not by lulling over and over in my mind
Mindless waves on an endlessly dormant sea
But by thought, determination, discussion, debate
Where this world takes us isn't up to fate
Luck was a concept invented only to cover up for our mistakes

To take away some of the blame
But we all know
We all know
That we're all a part of this.

We're all a part of this mess
Yes, at best, a mess
A tip
A trashcan
We all play a part
But we can all play a part
In fixing
Cleaning
Tidying
Unfolding
Developing
Discussing
Debating
Welcoming equality for you and for me
Taking away the endless burden of an unspoken dream
We know we want it badly, so what's stopping us?

That's the only question
What's stopping us?
What's slowing us down?

Why?
Why am I not considered equal to a man? Why are there more men named John in positions of authority in business than women overall?

(statistics don't lie, even maths proves the world isn't cured of prejudice yet)
And why?
What is the point? Where does it lead?
Are we just walking nowhere, being led on and on by owners like dogs on leads?

In my dream, not asleep, not in bed, not at night
In my head, in my mind
My calculated wish—more than a wish
My plan
In my plan, we achieve equality

You know you agree you want it just as bad as I. Not the same. But equal
So
What's
Stopping us?

Emma Archer (13)

Nature's Cry

Watching and waiting
Hopeless and lost
Guided with misfortune
Grievance
And loss

Wailing and crying
Tears of distress
As nature experiences massive unrest
While nature cries humanity sleeps

In pain and suffering
Light comes forth
As revolutions in our heads spring forth
As nature rejoices at
Humanity's choice

To sleep above the ocean bed
With winds and whistles overhead
To unite our seas within our nations
And claim our skies in desperation
All in the name of peace and love
Against a crisis we should rise above.

Micaiah Williams (16)

I Had A Dream

I had a dream, that one day I could leave this cage.
That I could somehow bend the bars that suffocated me and wriggle out.
That once I left, I would soar and run and never stop. Ever.
But that was a long time ago, when I didn't know how deep the poison had seeped in,
when I didn't realise how cramped my cage was,
when I blamed myself for not being able to breathe,
when I cried over every little pain, every injustice, every cut and scar and bruise that strangely, only I could feel,
when I believed those who were really my captors, were the only ones who wouldn't leave me.
When;
the manipulation,
the fear of having nobody else,
the pressure,
the inconsistent patterns of pain and praise,
the confusion,
the constant fear of ending up on the streets or some other horrible fate if I shared this secret, forcing my obedience,
the knowledge nowhere else would be the same, snatching my voice without me realising,
the never-dying thirst for validation,
was the only life I'd ever known.

And when people try to talk to me about mental health, I pretend to care, so that nobody would think I needed 'help',

because I'd been trained to believe that I would be dragged into some cruel foster home the moment I opened my mouth.
But on the inside, I think:
Is that a joke?! Of course, my opinion doesn't matter. It never has and never will.
Depression? I don't know what that is. Oh, you mean weakness, yeah, I'm not allowed to have that.
Trauma? No, why would I have that, it's not like I matter enough to have emotions.
My life was like a performance, except for the fact that it wasn't mine. I existed for the sole benefit of others.
Someone people could compare their children to, to redirect the guilt of their lousy parenting onto their child's flaws,
Someone educators could brag about, to make themselves look useful,
Someone relatives could proudly announce they were related to, so that no one would notice their own shortcomings.
They thought I had it all.
But did I really though?
When the constant competition to outdo myself, each time slowly made my emotions deteriorate away,
making me more and more obsessed with other's opinions because I didn't have any of my own.
That's how it went on and on and on in an infinite cycle.
Funny how people can flake on you,
the second you fail to live up to their expectations, which is technically your own fault.

Because who set those expectations in the first place?
Then feeling guilty for not being good enough to be paraded around like a trophy. A never-ending loop.
And you wanna know what the worst bit is, the interrogations.
"What happened?"
"Why can't you be like before?"
I know it doesn't seem like much. But these two questions are the title of my past.
Do you know why it hurts?
Because the questioners pretend like they actually care, when really, they're just looking for the quickest way to fix their broken product.
And worse than that, I can't tell them it was all a lie. That's right. I acted dumb, because it was the only way out of that endless cycle.
The humiliation, when someone treats me like less, is unimaginable,
They think they're better than me when I know for a fact, I could outdo them in my sleep.
But I stay silent, because I've learnt from experience, that silence makes the present less painful.
This, this is the reason I don't dream.
This is why I never question why I feel happier away from my reality and focus on the guilt, that I'm supposed to feel, because after all, they had 'sacrificed everything for me' (even though I never asked them to).
And if you're thinking I don't dream because my dreams were shattered, you'd be wrong.

Because I HAD a dream, and that dream came true.
I grew out of my cage.
But I don't run, I walk,
I don't soar,
I stop and cry, and cry and cry even when it feels like I've run out of tears.
Because it is exhausting trying to heal, when you're still in chains.

Joan Jeswin (13)

The Robots Game

Dear Diary,
I am Austin, a normal kid who loves playing video games, but today, that all changed. I was riding my bike down the road, only to find three roads closed all in one place. I had no choice but to turn back. I was looking around the place to see why it was closed but nothing added up. Then I saw it, a robot; I rubbed my eyes to make sure I was awake. I was shocked by the sight. My mouth hung open, and I immediately took my phone out to take a picture. No battery. *I specifically remember charging my phone to 100%, why does it all of a sudden not work?* Then 'it' saw me. I had been seen. My heart dropped. I hopped on my bike and pedalled as fast as I could. It wasn't chasing me, which was a good sign. It was staring at me as I pedalled away. I tried not to focus on it, but that was nearly impossible. I was close to my house, and then I heard it. *Was it a scream or a roar? Or maybe a shout?*
I was three minutes away from my house. The ten-foot-tall robot was out of my sight. I ran to my doorstep and pulled out my keys. I quickly opened the door and ran to my aunty, who takes care of me because my parents passed away. I hugged her and told her to look out the window while I went upstairs to get my camera. She asked, "Why, hun?"
I said, "Just look," and she went to the window. She gasped loudly. I ran to her. She ran as far away from the window. I tried to explain, but she shouted, "What was that?" Before I could speak, she splashed water on her face to calm herself down and make sure she wasn't dreaming.

I told her it was a robot and that I saw it on the way back. It kept staring, like it knew me from somewhere. I kept thinking, but nothing clicked. I don't even remember what happened yesterday, like my memory was wiped. My brain was definitely trying to tell me something, but I couldn't tell what it was.

Suddenly, the house shook, and I was scared. I pulled out my phone, but I realised it wasn't charged. It turned on. *How did that happen? I definitely remember my phone being out of charge. How does it work now?* While I was trying to find out the solution to this, the house shook again. My aunt screamed and grabbed the closest sharp object, which happened to be a fork. She aimed it at the window. I ran down after I heard the scream and saw 'it'. *How did it know where I was?* I ran outside to see it. It made a loud screech. I was surprisingly not scared. *Why?* I felt a sensation in my stomach. Butterflies. The feeling you feel on a drop of a roller coaster. I trusted it. My aunt saw all of this and screamed. Loud. I ran to her and gave her a hug. I went back to the animatronic.

A few days later, I was brought all the way to America, to San Francisco, and then to Lombard Street. It didn't know how to walk up with all the turns, so it had to find another way to go. I woke up and the animatronic had food. Human food, a whole platter (burgers, chips, sauces, pizza, ice cream). It had every kid's dream. I was a vegetarian, but somehow it knew that, as if it had scanned me. Or did it know me? I started to realise, *this robot looks oddly familiar*. It looked exactly like the same one in the game I used to play at home (Robot Wars). *Was it the same one? It can't be. Robots aren't real.*

I was right. I was on my computer for so long that it started to gravitate me towards the game. Until I got sucked into the game. I got taken into the game and didn't realise it. That's why my aunt screamed, she saw me in the game! How did I end up in San Francisco? The game has many modes, all in different areas in the world, so I was on Earth, but not my Earth. That's when I realised this wasn't a dream, *this is reality.*

Hassan Khan (12)

I Have A Dream

I have a dream where poverty isn't a thing.
I have a dream where we all blend, treating each other like the kings and queens we are.
I have a dream where we are no longer dominated, but we dominate the radah that was given to us in the Genesis of life. The dominion that was snatched from us has been restored. And in that dream, it turned into reality. We all had wealth. We all lived like heaven was on Earth.
I have a dream where we all live abundantly, exceedingly more than we could ever imagine.
I have a dream where we don't lack but take care of each other.
I have a dream where we love each other, not for personal gain, but because it's in our hearts.
I have a dream where we seek first the true Priorities.
I have a dream where we are all one. Where we exercise our royalty.
I have a dream where it's all clean. Where trauma is gone, vanished, and love is the only language left.
I have a dream where borders don't bind us, where papers can't limit us, where we touch the heights we were meant to reach.
I have a dream where we live unlimited. Where heaven is the limit, not the sky, even while on Earth. The Kingdom Way. But when will we finally make that dream a reality?

Victor Alyanyi (17)

Dream

They asked me to write about my dream. Oh, where do I start now?
He sits down on his bed. A bed placed at the corner of a room about the size of a jail cell. It's not exactly a bed but two mattresses and a dark blue bedsheet on top, desperately trying to place the mirage of a bed. The bed is placed beside a grey table and a black chair.
What he set out to make, an organised study workspace, became a colourless, soulless and forgotten storage space, complete with an odd black chair. It looked hideous—laughable compared to what he imagined. A window overlooking the road seems to be the only connection with reality he has. Cars occasionally pass by and people chat away. He lies down in his bed and closes his eyes to enter his real world where he can do anything. His dream world looks like him waking up in a well-made house complete with mahogany furniture, a garage hosting a suite of his favourite cars and—most importantly—people who love him. He leaves for work at nine after eating a breakfast of Turkish eggs and coffee. He walks into the country's best hospital after parking his sports car outside, as he puts on a green lanyard proudly displaying his name with a celebrated prefix of Dr. He greets his fellow surgeons and after logging on to his computer, starts planning the surgery of a patient coming that day.
His room at work houses a high-end computer kept on a fairly large table with a black office chair. A small window over the table provides just enough sunlight to go by.

Though the room is not very snazzy, his real workplace is the operation theatre down at the other end of the corridor. To the world, an eerie place with the doors resembling guards at the face of such a hell which some don't survive. Over the menacing doors is a blood-red sign reading *Operation Theatre* and a red light only switched on when someone is fighting for their life inside. However, to him, it's any other day at work.

He puts on his anti-contamination kit to keep the theatre germ-free and enters a dark room with a single light lit above a person who has been an unfortunate victim of a brutal car crash. He walks in to be greeted by a team of the best operation theatre staff and begins an operation which could save someone from disastrous consequences. Five hours on, he walks out of the chamber and warmly greets the patient's family, informing them of the good news that the patient shall make a speedy recovery. As a kind gesture, a little girl from the family gives him a thank-you card for saving her father's life. He gets down on a knee and accepts it, thanking the girl as well.

His day goes by saving lives and he returns home at six in the evening. Later, he goes to meet a car fanatic in the city to record a collaboration video for his successful YouTube channel about cars. They review and race the two fastest cars on the planet, testing them in racing, looks, safety and many more crucial aspects that make them the best in the world.

After a tiring day, he drives home in a sports SUV listening to a podcast about time management. After a light dinner of a potato sandwich and a thrilling motorsport race on TV, he slams down on the bed to rest after a day of hard endeavours.

Moments later, his actual self wakes up, who is still in high school, aspiring to be successful. But whether it be high school, university or a hospital, he will stop nowhere. That boy wants it. That boy craves it. That boy needs it! He feels it! It's his motivation! It's his dream! And he is me.

Mohammad Mashhood (13)

A Dream Like No Other

I have a dream, a dream like no others but it still helps me in some way.
I have a dream, not to go to space or be in movies like some expect me to say.
My dreams so simple yet complicated. So easy yet hard to achieve
And sometimes I think I'm silly to believe
That my perfect little dream will ever come true
But I try because I know it'll be worth it if I do.
My dream, my silly little dream that I dream at night
Is to win my constant, overwhelming fight,
One without fists or an audience, dodging or aggression
But one with injury's anxiety and a constant depression.
A battle no one sees, that it drains me every day,
One that everyone lives through but they won't say,
One where the thoughts spiral round and round,
One where there's no peace to be found,
One where life gets the best of me,
One that I'm not sure I'll ever be free.
But my dream keeps me going in some way,
That hope that I won't feel like this one day.
So I dream, and I fight, and I quietly pray,
That this storm in my soul will pass one day.
And maybe that dream, so small yet bright,
Will guide me gently back to light.

Jacey Warhurst-Green (17)

The Sky Is Blue

The sky is blue
Raise your eye to the sky
And never wonder why
The sky is blue
It's a known truth
Something we never question
We don't need a lesson
To tell us something we see just outside the windows
But the truth is the sky isn't blue though
Of deep night, the sky's like looking into space
An endless black with speckled stars that shoot off and race
And of the sun's first glance, the sky's a muted rainbow as it ascends
It runs across both ends
From deep orange to pale pink
But in the end we barely blink
We still say the sky is blue, that's a fact
We just accept it, why is that?
I notice now how much we just accept without a reason why
Like sometimes it's okay to lie
But lying is a sin, we're told as a child never to lie, and yet sometimes it's fine
Or we just accept that people may not like us
They may try to push and shove

And make you fit with their perfect vision
But we never ask why they choose this mission
I'm not allowed to ask why it is you don't like me
They'll never answer with full honesty
I'll never know why I'm so awful to you
But there's nothing I can do
I just have to accept your opinion, which to you is a fact
The fact that your smiles are just an act
We are taught tears mean sad and smiles are good
But fake smiles mess your logic up
I see them smile, I don't ask why
I'll never know if it's the truth or another lie
Because we just accept it if we are told so many times
So what seems like fact could be a lie
Or maybe it all depends on where you are
After all, only some of the world sees stars
Maybe where I am the sky is blue
However, it's different for you
Our truths are built on perspective
Which makes the truth elective
Is any fact 100% true?
Well, science would curse me for this truth
And say that if I do something enough
And the outcome is such
Then how can I think that it's a lie?
Well, I smile every day but do my eyes?
I wash my hands but will they ever be 100% clean?

People who are mean, are they only mean?
Humans and science they don't mix well
Even though there's a whole science to tell
That it's science, the reason behind everything
But in science, it's hard to prove anything
I cannot see your particles so I take your word
But what if I misheard
Just one simple word
Then that truth is not true
And was it me or you?
Whose conscience does this sin rest on?
Did any of us do anything wrong?
I could never conclude this argument
Because there is no point
But I know that truth depends on perspective
And truth is elective
So when you tell me the sky is blue
Though that may be the case for you
I'll tell you no from where I stand
The sky is not blue, maybe golden like sand
And that's okay
And maybe one day
You'll see this golden sky
And if I don't see it that day, you can tell me what you see in the sky
Until one day we'll meet eye to eye
A perfect day under a gold scene

That's my dream
So I raise my eye to the sky
And instead of wondering why
I wonder what the sky looks like to you.

Taylor Bennett (15)

Softly

"What do you dream about?"
She asks,
Softly.
Staring at the ceiling above,
The blankets pulled tight,
Covering her frail little body,
Like the arms of her
Sister.
"I dream about..."
I whisper,
Softly.
Like a small mouse,
Squeaking out the words,
So insignificant.
"That one day when I wake up I'll be
A superhero."
She laughs so
Melancholic and
Sorrowful
I think she could be
Crying.
"Oh."
She breathes after a while,
Softly.
Glow-in-the-dark stars light up the walls,
A galaxy before her,

And yet she
Cries,
Softly.
"I dream of being home again."
She chokes back the sobs,
The sadness.
My eyebrows shoot up
Like rockets.
The walls that enclose us are
Hers.
The teddies and dolls surrounding us are
Hers.
She's home.
"You are,"
I state,
Softly.
She shakes her head slowly.
I watch her eyes gaze over the room,
The books, the toys, her
Art.
Taking in the wonder of childhood,
The beauty of living
As a kid.
She's so pale though, like a
Ghost.
Her eyes so round like a
Child's.

Her voice so soft like a
Memory.
"You are home,"
I repeat,
Not so softly.
Again, there's this slow shake of her
Head.
"You are,"
I press,
Urgently.
Those grey eyes look so
Doll like,
The hair like
Yarn.
"You are!"
I shout,
Harshly.
But she's
Gone.
Vanished and replaced with a little
Doll.
Lifeless and small,
Wrapped in blankets that
Cradle her,
Like a river flowing around her little
Neck,
Tucking her little arms

Away,
Leaving her little face,
So pure and
Unreal
To stare back at me.
Until a hand touches my shoulder,
A gentle voice
Of hope,
"Wake up,"
She says,
Softly.
Blinding fluorescent lights wake me
From my dream.
And a nurse stands there,
Holding my hand.
My hand,
So wrinkled and worn down like an
Old tree
In my garden
That aged with me
And her.
There's this heavy weight that seems to
Rest on me
Of a life
Lived.
A long life of
Joy and

Loss.
"Had a nice dream?"
She asks,
Softly.
Closing my eyes, I breathe a
Slow breath.
"Yes,"
I say,
Softly.
And I picture her in an empty bed next to
Mine,
That sweet, young
Doll face.
And let the beeps of the monitor
Beep their final
Breaths
Too.

Samantha Morrison (16)

A Voice In The Storm

A voice in the storm is all that is left.
Against the booming waves and the pitch-black sky, the lighthouse can't find its way to me.
I didn't have any armour, but I had my voice.
I knew no one could hear me, but I screamed anyway.
A tiny part of me refused to give up with all I have been through.
Many people would've given up by now and that 1% who wouldn't keep on going.
And that's what my father called me.
The 1% that kept on going, no matter the circumstances and no matter how badly I wanted to give up.
I look hastily for any sign of living but my voice against the storm is all that I have.
But a light in me shines, one that I've not seen before.
The more I try to give up, the brighter it gets.
Slowly but surely, it embraces my soul.
It consumes me with the tiny hope I once had before it vanished and now turned into a massive flame, not bright but a hopeful one.
One strong enough that it will make me stand until the storm dies out.
I have a voice.
A powerful and strong one.
And one that will make me go against the storm and anything that goes against me.

Brittany Scarlet Vargas-Torres (13)

When The World Is Asleep

When the whole world is asleep,
I walk up the ribs of the moon,
barefoot on light.
While the sky buzzes in my ears like heartbeat,
And wishes I whisper into the dark –
not prayers, not plans, only little sparks
that are trying to find a way home.

Down there,
the city is folded like paper -
dreams tucked between its creases:
a boy drawing wings
on the back of a detention slip,
a girl teaching herself how to sing
without anyone's permission,
a mother dreaming in two languages
and an old streetlight that won't
stop shining.

I dream too.
Not palaces or praise,
but mornings that don't hurt to wake in,
voices that don't need to shout to be heard,
hands that build not break.

I dream of oceans that forgive us
for everything we have thrown inside them,

of forests that breathe once more,
of faces that fear hasn't blurred.

In one dream,
I am older -
not by years but by understanding.

The mirror doesn't ask
who I'm supposed to be;
it listens,
like an old friend.
I see the map.

In a different dream,
the stars consist of letters,
and the cosmos spell out 'begin again'.
Kids are running after comets,
chalk-stained fingers advancing
futures on night walls.
Even silence feels alive,
a promise to be uttered.

But dreams are a soft thing.
They can slip right through you like rain,
and too tight you hold, too slow you slip.
Morning arrives,
and the alarm lops the moon off.
The real world yawns open,
ask for proof.

Still,
I carry a spark in my sleeve.
I tuck it into books,
feed it soft breaths,
train it to glow without apology.
And when the world falls asleep
to what dreaming feels like,
I'll light it again.

Because I've learned this:
dreaming is not a place you go.
It is a language
you learn to speak,
one hope at a time.
And maybe if we all spoke it,
louder than the doubt,
softer than the hate,
maybe the world wakes
to find itself
rebirthed,
breathing itself in colour,
standing in its own light.

When the world is asleep,
I am wide awake,
watching the future turn

Not forced to eat plastic,
Not burned all over.
No one would cut her hair.
Would she not be doused in oil?
Or filled with metal,
Shoved into her skin.

This will never happen,
Or if I'm mistaken, we could be like the Lorax:
UNLESS.
Unless we act now, there'll be nothing to act on.
No seas or beautiful skies.
No, unless we act now, there'll be nothing to breathe.
And our loving mothers shall die.

Our world is already on fire,
But it's not too late to fix.
We're getting there; yes.
But trust—there's still time.
Little time there is:
But whatever time shall remain
Is better than having none.

So help fix it today,
Find a charity for a bay!
Any and everything counts.

A penny or pound,
It all helps a bound.

To save our world from the fire.

To save our girl—Mother Nature,
Is that all we should live for?
We stand on her Earth; we must be kind.
For generations ago, a grave mistake...
One that could end us was made;
We set our world on fire.

Let's fix it,
Mix it.
Not blur it into the past—for to remember and learn is a priority.
But let's make Earth green again,
For our futures before us.

#LongLiveEarth.

Evie Chapman (14)

A Girl's Dream

My dream last night was not something made up
Instead, my eyes fluttered open to the pink walls
Of the bedroom I had decorated when I was six
Glitter, teddies and unicorns all in the mix
The door cracked open, and my brother's head popped round
He asked me to come down to have breakfast with him
I slid my feet into my slippers and bumped down the stairs
Looking at the array of cereals made me happy, not scared
Little marshmallows and puffed rice mounted in our bowls
Glug went the milk as it splashed down and around
I dug my spoon in and shovelled it into my lips
Without a second thought as to how it would affect my hips
When I woke up, my heart sank at my new stark white room
With a scattering of posters of artists I didn't even like
My parents asked if I wanted something to eat
I said no, I was no longer the girl who could go with the flow
My heart yearns for the small free spirit I once was
The sassy diva who did as she pleased
Could fuel her body before bones started to protrude
A girl who wasn't scared of what she saw when she was nude.

F M H (18)

When I Grow Up

When I grow up, will I travel?
Will I soar through the skies
Or will I swim through the sea
From fish to fish
To wish to wish
When I grow up?

When I grow up, will I have fun?
Maybe do a charity run
Or jog around the park on a sunny day
But watch TV on a rainy one
I wonder if I'll be the fun person in the group
When I grow up

When I grow up, will I be rich?
Money from working hard at my job
When I cry, money will be at the ready
Morning, evening, night or in Spain
Shopping at malls will make me feel okay
When I grow up

When I grow up, will I be kind?
Donate to the poor
Or be a doctor and help all of those patients in pain
And what will I gain?
A planet of smiling people who will know my name
When I grow up

When I grow up, will I save?
Help achieve world peace
Or be a superhero
Flying away to save another day
And I will help and do what I can
When I grow up

When I grow up, will I still write?
Be a poet, an author, or a star
I may dedicate my books to the ones I love
My family, my friends, my broken guitar
And especially my best friend who has moved away very far
When I grow up

When I grow up, will I sing?
High notes, low notes
A song called the ring
Beatboxing, rapping
Or just a simple singer
When I grow up

When I grow up, will I be me?
A silly, goofy little girl
Who hopes to believe
To learn and learn
Until I can't
When will that be?
I'm not too sure

Until I reach that destination, I will continue to open some doors
I may think to stop on a really rainy day
But I'm sure that I will always overcome and always try
And time and time, I have proven to myself
That I'm brave, young and beautiful
And will always be
Unless I fall down the path of bad decisions
And end up with a heart oh so empty
Which I won't
When I grow up.

Miruna Nimalathasan (12)

Dreams Are Most Peculiar

D reams are the most peculiar things,
R eplaying your day back to you,
E verything warped and altered,
A ll similar but not quite the same,
M aybe it's our mind's way of coping,
S tress relief?

A re dreams about our innermost desires?
R evealing our hidden wants and truths,
E verything spread out in our own minds.

M ostly we have average dreams about everyday things,
O r we have scary dreams with our most fearsome monsters,
S ometimes we dream about what we want the most,
T hings that we have never told a soul.

P ersonally, my dreams are quite odd,
E arth being taken over by noodle aliens in pea-ships,
C old plunges in the river, pushed by the sadistic wind,
U ltimate dreams of fear and elation,
L ike getting 100% on a test, only to find you're naked!
I n some dreams I remember things,
A ge-old memories that I thought I forgot,
R eally, dreams are super weird—anything could happen!

Blake Smith (15)

My Distant Dreams

If you were to ask about my dreams,
You might expect the usual fame or cars,
Maybe something bolder like an astronaut,
Dreaming to explore planets like Mars,
But that which many take for granted,
Like health and a peaceful home,
That is what I crave the most,
Every day in my thoughts all alone,
I hope to overcome this anxiety,
To enjoy a peace of mind,
To be stronger than my OCD,
Leaving these intrusive thoughts behind,
If that's too good to be true,
Then I hope it's easy with them to co-exist,
I dream of being resilient and in control,
Not barely being able to resist,
I hope to laugh at these whispers,
Not feel overwhelmed or fear,
To tell these compulsions I won't listen,
To take back control in my life and steer,
I hope to move past letters and doctors,
To make my parents not worried but proud,
To have quiet and comfortable success,
It doesn't have to be loud!
I dream of being purposeful,
I hope to finally have found my way,

To feel ready when questioned by family,
Having more about myself to say,
I dream to no longer avoid mirrors,
For my hair to no longer drive me mad,
I hope to admire my looks like others,
Instead of it making me feel sad,
I don't want to feel behind anymore,
Every time I look and see the date,
No more shadow of avoided problems,
Making me feel for myself hate,
I want it to be my turn to celebrate,
I too want to get married and settle down,
I want to laugh with my whole heart,
Without following it with a frown,
I hope one day again,
My shoulders will feel light,
My breathing will be more of a pleasure,
My eyes will finally shine bright,
For I dream of living instead of surviving,
No more inner conflict, no more war,
I want my existence to feel like a privilege,
Not a burden or a chore.

Badar Ahmed (18)

What They Tried To Burn

I come from the land of rivers and six seasons,
Bangladesh, if you will.
The one with the sweetest tongue,
The one that fought for its voice—and won.
The one whose fabric, softer than air, draped itself
through rings and across empires.
But none of it came free. Not without cost.
That beautiful language, spoken by millions with love now,
was protected by the blood of martyrs, young lives lost,
so we could speak our truth,
so we could honour the mothers who raised us,
with a day born not from flowers,
but from fire and courage.
And that fabric, the muslin so fine, it floated like mist,
was torn apart by greed, burned away by foreign hands,
who feared its beauty more than they feared war.
And when the famine came,
it wasn't just the sky that failed us.
It was the men in power.
While rice spoiled in storage,
three million ghosts walked our shores,
and silence screamed louder than mercy.
Yet, they called us a curse.
They called us weak.
As if we hadn't bled just to speak our birthright.
As if our history wasn't cut, ripped, stitched, and stolen.

As if my ancestors weren't starved
by their so-called 'heroes'.
And still, we became
one of the fastest-growing economies in Asia,
building with hands once bruised,
dreaming in a language they once tried to erase.
We hold the longest sea beach in the world,
where the sun kisses both dawn and dusk.
We shelter the largest mangrove forest,
where the Royal Bengal Tiger walks like a king,
where deer leap, and rivers sing.
So, if they ask where I'm from, I can say it proudly,
I come from a land that blossoms even after the fire.
The land that turned its scars into its strength,
Made from rivers, rebellions, and remembrance,
Bangladesh.

Ameera Akthar-Alim

Still, I Dream

I have a dream
but no one listens.
It slips from me,
fragile as glass,
and breaks in their silence.

They say, "just try, it's enough",
but when the silence cracks,
old failures come crawling back,
named, counted,
laid bare at my feet like sins.

I keep pushing
because I want to be the one
who makes the path smoother,
who stands tall enough
to hold up the sky.
because they all deserve ease,
and I am meant to be strong.

But sometimes,
the weight is more than I can hold.

I have a dream
that my words will matter,
that my voice is not forgotten
two minutes after it leaves my lips,

that every effort is not a ghost
vanishing into nothing.

I have a dream
that the pieces of me
I sacrifice in silence—
sleep, joy,
the little things I loved—
are not overlooked,
are not forgotten,
are not wasted.

But here I stand,
hands trembling,
heart bruised,
and nothing is enough.
Still, I dream.

I dream of pride and warmth
that does not vanish when tempers flare.
Not borrowed, not conditional,
not handed to others while I stand bare.

I dream of being free
from the endless trial
of proving myself
again, and again, and again.

But I wake, instead,
to fault-finding shadows,

to the quiet cruelty
of never enough.

So, I stop speaking,
I stop hoping out loud.
My voice dissolves into silence,
my sacrifice into air.

Yet still,
in the darkest corners of me,
I clutch this fragile dream
that one day,
what I give,
will be enough.

That one day,
someone will see me
and not turn me away.

Riddhikaa Vidyakumar (15)

Rolamia: A Dream Unfolding

I dream not in fragments, but in galaxies,
each thought a constellation,
each hope a star burning bright
in the firmament of Rolamia,
my world beyond the reach of waking.
There, the air tastes like possibility,
sweet as sunlit nectar dripping from golden vines.
The trees hum lullabies in languages lost,
and their roots braid stories into the soil.
The moon is no mere orb,
but a silver compass guiding dreamers home.
Its craters cradle my ambitions,
each one a cradle for the impossible.
In Rolamia, I am not small. I am seismic,
a force that bends time like willow branches in the wind.
I speak, and mountains lean in to listen.
My fears dissolve like ink in rain,
and courage blooms in fields of fireflowers,
their petals flickering with the light
of every 'what if' I dared to believe.
Rolamia is not escape. It is a blueprint.
A map etched in metaphor,
leading me from who I am to who I might become.
So let them scoff at dreams too vast to measure.
I know the truth: Rolamia lives in me, and I,
I am its beating heart.

Khudeeja Begum (18)

A Voice Lost

I used to blend into the crowd,
just another face in a sea of sameness,
until high school's harsh spotlight
struck like lightning in a storm,
and revealed a truth I wasn't ready to hold.
My difference—sudden, heavy,
tore through me like wind through fractured glass.

Others spoke with effortless grace,
their words dancing like swans on summer lakes,
while my own throat stayed bound
by chains no one else could see.
Each attempt at speech
was a battle against myself,
my mind, a stubborn gatekeeper,
denying me peace.

I pleaded with it:
Let me be.
But every day, the voices returned:
"*Naive girl,*" they whispered,
echoes of a time I was too blind to notice
false smiles
and jokes that only made sense to them.

I wasn't just the only one not laughing,
I was the only one drowning.

The pain began to settle in,
slow and acidic,
as cruel games played out like tic-tac-toe
meant only for my humiliation.
And with each mark on that invisible board,
shame carved deeper into my chest.

A storm brewed within me.
I wanted to swim out, to rise above the waves,
but I only sank further.
Each tear another tide,
each breath a silent scream
for a voice I couldn't find.

Eyes turned toward me,
expectant, impatient.
Their silence roared louder than words,
like lions crouched before a kill.
No protest dared leave my lips.
The chains of doubt held them captive,
each link forged in fear.

I became a prisoner
of my own insecurities,
a cage without bars,
a scar without blood,
invisible to the world
but impossible to unfeel.

Priscilla-Grace Aina (15)

The Weight Of What It Is

Dreams are like paper lanterns,
Fragile, burning bright,
Released into the midnight air,
Snuffed before they find their height.

They said be anything you want,
But stitched in me is a frame;
Boys are strong, girls are soft,
A script I never claimed.
The chorus of stereotype,
Still echoes through the hall.
But freedom feels like silence,
Not being named at all.

In rooms of steel and silence,
A surgeon's hand still shakes,
The scalpel sings of miracles,
But not all wounds can break.
Hope lies, breathing, fading fast.
And prayers turn into cries.
Sometimes even gods in scrubs,
Must learn that someone dies.

Feminism is marching,
With trainers, heels and scars.
Climbing through a ceiling,
That still rains down its shards.

Equality is not handed,
It is clawed with blistered hands;
The bruises line our history.
But still, we choose to stand.

I wish I was a river,
To wash your grief away.
To take the roots of your trauma,
And throw them in the bay.
But sorrow clings like ivy.
Its tendrils will never let go.
I will hold what weight I'm able,
The rest I cannot throw.

Reality is a teacher,
Its lessons cut like glass;
Dreams bend until they splinter.
Too fragile, here, to last.
And yet within the breaking,
A glimmer still remains,
The fragments shine like warnings,
Or stars, inside the pain.

And still,
I don't know what the future holds.
It could be storm,
It could be silence,
It could be something I've never met before.

But I am here,
And I will meet it.
With whatever I have left to give.

Hallie Whitmore-Bond (15)

Marine Biology

I have autism, a unique way to see,
a world of wonders calling out to me.
In the deep blue ocean, where the dolphins play,
I dream of being brave, and swimming far away.

Coral reefs in colours, bright and full of cheer,
with every wave that whispers, I feel them draw near.
I watch the graceful fish, how they dart and glide,
in my heart, I know, there's magic in the tide.

Beneath the surface calm, a secret world awaits,
with turtles gliding slow and mysterious gateways.
I want to learn their stories, to understand their song,
to care for every creature, to help where I belong.

The ocean's vast and endless, I dream to explore,
with knowledge in my hands, I will open every door.
To study every echo, to protect what is so dear,
to be a marine biologist, to chase away the fear.

I have autism, my heart beats strong and true,
with my dreams of ocean wonders, I know what I will do.
A future filled with purpose, beneath the sun's bright
beams,
I will make a splash for all, fulfilling all my dreams.

Caitlin Atkin (17)

Dreams In My Backpack

I zip up my bag, it's September again,
New shoes, new pens, a head full of rain.
Year Eight now, somehow I'm taller and my school friends are too,
But school still smells like paper and that shiny floor shiner.
This summer was different, not beaches and sun,
But a summer of protesting and street marchers that did make a sound.
I watched on television as the peaceful masses walked down the streets,
They marched for their voices and marched for their dreams.
They marched in the sun and they marched in the rain,
Holding up placards that didn't read all the same.
I saw people marching in London and all over the world,
With posters and hope, some jovial, some bold.
They shouted for world peace and for kids just like I.
Some shouting were kids, and their voices so high.
I dreamt of all that happened during summer,
And I dreamt of kids around the world, happy like I,
I dreamt of marchers singing happy songs as they went on by.
Dreams, lots of dreams,
"Oh, where do I put them all?
I know, I know! My zipped backpack might fit them all."
"Hurry, it's time for school," my mum, Natasha May Mambwe-Mwananshiku, says to me,

"Let's get to the car," my dad, Martin Mwananshiku, says,
"or the traffic will be as heavy as can be."
Now I'm back in school, and the bell starts to ring,
But I still hear the summer, it taught me a thing:
That dreams aren't just night-thoughts that might slip away,
They're marches and voices and visions that stay.
So I carry my dreams in my backpack each day,
Next to my lunch and my Year Eight display, reading
'Amana Mary Mwananshiku, Summer of 2025'.

Amana Mwananshiku (12)

A Future Where I Was Free

I had this dream
A dream where I felt free
A dream where I found reasons to always beam
This made me feel as free as a bee
No one stood in front of my path
No more lies, no more sadness
The prison bars which kept me in agony
I was finally free...
The tears finally came to an end
All that was left was a confident grin
No more foes, just friends
I stood up with my chin up high
A future where I was proud of me
I was done letting people down
For the first time, I flew and didn't flee
For the first time, I saw people proud of me
No more looking down and nasty frowns
Just me...
A world where I could be who I really was
A world where I didn't need to lie to satisfy people
No more rules that held me back for who I was
Just a nice person was left of me, I wasn't evil
This didn't feel like the end to me
This felt like a fresh start
A start where I laughed endlessly
I finally was able to say things by heart

I meant the things I said
A dream where I didn't care about how much money would make me rich
A dream where I wasn't cold-hearted
A dream where I was kind
And most importantly, I was free from all worries
A future where people looked up to me
A future where I became the person who I always wanted to be
Where I met all expectations
And where I met all standards
I earned my respect
I earned my self-worth
I earned my happiness
And most importantly earned my freedom
This is my dream
A dream I want to accomplish
A dream to be free
A dream to be me
No more insecurities
No more pain
My dream is to be free.

Jivisha Garg (12)

I Have A Dream (About Peace)

I have a dream the world can heal,
Where kindness cuts sharper than iron or steel.
Where no child wakes to the sound of fear,
And every voice is safe to hear.

I dream of lands without a line,
Where hearts are flags and all souls shine.
Where colours are cherished, not cause for hate,
And peace is not left to chance or fate.

I have a dream where silence is sweet,
Not the hush of war beneath retreat.
Where drums are played, not beaten in fight,
And daybreak always follows night.

I dream of leaders bold and wise,
Who look through truth, not polished lies.
Who trade their power not for gold,
But for a future brave and bold.

I have a dream of open hands,
Of building bridges, not making demands.
Where weapons rust in fields of grain,
And no one learns to kill again.

I dream of cities lit by grace,
Where strangers smile face to face.

Where no one flees, no one hides,
And peace walks proudly on all sides.

I have a dream that war will cease,
Not just a pause, but lasting peace.
Not silence drawn from fear or chains,
But harmony that still remains.

I dream of children planting trees,
Instead of bombs beneath their knees.
Of lullabies in every tongue,
And songs that teach what's yet unsung.

I have a dream the earth will mend,
That peace begins where we extend.
A hand, a word, a simple start,
A dream that lives in every heart.

And if we dare, and if we try,
If we lift our eyes beyond the sky,
Then maybe peace is not a gleam,
But something real. I have that dream.

Joanna Chukwuoma John-Isaac (12)

I Have A Dream (From The In-Between)

They never tell you what it feels like to be between.
Not alive, not dead, not dreaming—but not quite awake.
They never say how empty the void is when the world forgets you.
When your name becomes silence.
When your body is gone, but your thoughts—never stop.
And yet, even there, adrift in the nothing, I dreamed.
Not of peace. Not of endings. But of return.
Of doing something with the second chance no one saw coming.
I dreamed of breath. Of aching lungs.
Of standing once more, sword in hand, not just to fight—but to protect.
I dreamed of saving someone. Anyone.
Of proving that one small girl with trembling hands could still matter.
And that dream—it cracked the darkness.
A whisper. A name. Mine. Aya.
I remembered it then—who I was.
What I wanted. Why I bled. And I returned.
So yes, I have a dream. Not wild. Not impossible.
But forged from that void that almost took me.
I dream of a world where courage isn't a death sentence.
Where truth doesn't get buried beneath silence and blood.
Where children don't stand alone before monsters.

I dream that my voice—quiet as it is—might ripple.
Might echo louder than fear.
That the ones who fall won't be forgotten.
That the ones who rise do so holding more than just weapons.
I dream of using every breath I've been given—not just to live, but to change something.
To light a match in all that dark.
To remind the world: even from the in-between, you can come back.
You can still dream. And dreams—they can save lives.
Even if it starts with saving your own.

Rachelle Lopoua (14)

Do They?

I have a dream, as do many,
Of peace, prosperity and wealth.
That's what everyone says, isn't it?
I dream of a happy life.
I dream of a healthy family.
I dream of a loving partner.
I dream, I dream, I dream.
But what about those who don't dream?
Those who struggle to think, create and speak.
Those who are so trapped in their own lives they don't have the time to breathe and relax and dream.
Too busy with the overbearing pressure of family drama.
Too busy with the need to prove yourself, only for it to never be enough.
Too busy,
Too busy,
Too busy.
I had a dream once.
One of a happy future, a big house with a big garden and a loving family who never fought.
But all dreams come to an end.
I wish they didn't believe me, I do.
Maybe, just maybe if they didn't,
I'd be able to think for myself.
Maybe I'd be able to take a deep breath and relax.
Maybe I wouldn't have to take sides or make the wrong choices.

Maybe I wouldn't be played like a puppet, pulled by the strings of its masters on and on.
Made to do this and look at that and smile and fix my face.
Maybe, just maybe, I could dream of those strings breaking.
Pinocchio did it, why can't I?
Run away, be free of these tight strings wrapped around my limbs and throat.
Have a big house with a happy family.
Relax. Breathe.
The thing is, Pinocchio is a story, and everyone's story ends differently.

One thing connects them all.
We both know what this is, don't we?
You just have to remember, dreams don't last forever.
Do they?

Chili-Blossom Entwistle Boydell (16)

D.R.E.A.M

I dream because Martin dreamed,
his voice a river,
his words a sky.
He said freedom like thunder,
he said justice like dawn,
and though they tried to silence him,
his dream still marches on.

I dream because Rosa sat down
so we could stand tall.
Because Harriet followed the North Star,
carrying futures through the night.
Because Malcolm lit fire in the hearts of the weary,
because Maya turned scars into flight.

I dream because Mandela bore chains,
yet his spirit broke walls.
Because Claudia Jones wrote Carnival into the streets,
because Olive Morris raised fists when the law would not.
Because Windrush docked with hands that healed a nation,
though the welcome was ice,
though the letters said go home.

Black history is a song
written in blood and brilliance.
A rhythm carried in shackles, a harmony born in pain, a chorus of voices-

thunder, gospel, whispers—
that refuse to fade.

I dream of classrooms
where our children find themselves in every page.
Of streets where skin is not a sentence,
but a sunrise.
Of futures where laughter is not armour,
where joy is not resistance,
where love is simply love.

We were the chains,
but we broke them.
We were the ashes,
but we burned brighter.
We were the dream denied,
but still,
we dream.

Because black history is not a shadow.
It is a lantern.
It is the dream and the dreamers.
It is the fire that carried us here.

And I,
I will keep dreaming,
until the world learns to wake.

Victoria Ekechukwu (13)

Last Night

Last night, I dreamed of something new,
A world that felt safe, kind, and true.
Where no one hurt, and no one cried,
And no one ever had to hide.
No one was bullied at their school,
No one was called names to be cool.
No bullies laughed, no whispers stung,
And kindness lived on every tongue.
I saw a school with open hearts,
Where pressure didn't tear us apart.
No late-night stress, no tired eyes,
No feeling lost behind fake smiles.
In this world, no cuts on skin,
No pain we're scared to speak within.
No masks to wear, no fake, I'm fine,
Just people saying, "You're not alone—you're mine."
No one was trapped inside their head,
Feeling they'd be better dead.
Just people there who really care,
Who show us love and say, "I'm here."
Girls were strong and boys could cry,
And no one ever questioned why.
Everyone could be real,
And talk about the things they feel.
No hate for skin that's dark or light,
No judging who is wrong or right.

We stood as equals, side by side,
With no more hate left to divide.
There was no war, no fight, no fear,
No angry shouts we didn't hear.
Just peace that grew like morning light,
And dreams that soared into the night.
Growing was hard, learning fast,
But we didn't feel tied to our past.
We found our voice, we found our spark,
A way to guide us through the dark.
So last night, I made a plan,
To help this dream the best I can.
And maybe we can make it true,
For me, for them, for us, for you.

Sophie Stuart (14)

Paintball

My heart races at every shot fired, my head pounding so much I can't even think.
I dash and run and dive through the terror and the screaming and the yelling and the crying.
My head pounds with fear of being shot, it courses through my veins and plagues my skin;
it's a disease I can't control, can't get rid of, can't predict.
I wish I had a soft vest, maybe a hard one to protect me.
Instead, I have the cloth of my T-shirt and the comfort and warmth of my sweatshirt.
My sweatshirt hugs me, it's desperate to provide comfort, warmth, it fails dramatically.
I'm not trained in combat, I wish I was.
I wish I could fight the bangs fired but I can't,
and it shouldn't have to be admired.
The world outside is such a dark hue.
Control is often an illusion. No one truly has full control.
No one truly has full power. No one truly has full truths told.
I wish I could go to those countries and make everything right.
Just to be able to see children and mothers no longer full of fright.
Reality hits me like a stun gun.
My body trembles as I'm carted off, shifted back on a boat.
I'm only cargo and the cranes that drag me persist with a reminder 'I'm alien'.

The word isn't foreign, it's the policies that are.
I can't escape who I am, my identity leaves me behind bars.
Only to remind myself, it's all in my head.
I'm just playing paintball. I wish I could comfort every child who cries,
but I remind myself again it's just paintball. It's all lies.

Xantia Clarkson (16)

What We've Done

A boy is beaten for his skin,
As if the shade of it
Were a crime he chose to carry.

A girl is hated for who she loves,
As if the simple act of loving
Were something to be punished.

A life is stolen in the dark,
A scream swallowed by the night,
Another name written
On cardboard signs,
Shaking in a crowd of tears.

How many mothers hold empty rooms,
Beds still made, shoes by the door-
Waiting for footsteps
That will never come home?

How many children learn
To hide themselves,
To shrink,
To whisper prayers that sound like,
"Please let me survive today."

We are not born this way
We are taught this way
Told that the shade of our skin defines the soul within

Told that love requires matching tones to be real
Divided into black and white,
Good and evil,
Dangerous and safe.
When will this end?
When will we see each other as one?
We are people, not clothes,
We don't get to choose what to wear.

People pretend not to see,
We scroll past pain,
Like it's just another picture,
Another headline,
But these are lives,
People, friends,
Sisters and brothers,
Daughters and sons,
Mothers and fathers,
Breathing once,
Now broken.

If love were louder than hate,
If hands reached out instead of striking,
Maybe we'd remember,
That we all bleed the same red,
And that no one should die,
Or be silenced,
For being exactly who they are.

Sophie Garabedian (13)

Dream Weaver

I dream when the lights go out, when my room is dark, lying in bed with nothing but thoughts roaming free in my mind each night.
Every night, I dream my way out.
Out of these walls. Out of the noise. Out of the people who don't believe in me.
Fifteen, and the world feels too small for the galaxies behind my eyes.
There's so much in my head, it's like the whole world's waiting to escape.
My bedroom walls fade like smoke when I begin to write.
Reality loosens its grip, I slip between the lines, into worlds of my own stories.
My mum says I'm young, she says these dreams belong in whispers, not in books.
But I have so much waiting, chapters calling, characters awaiting, a future humming under my skin.
I'm only fifteen, but my mind is older, racing through centuries of stories, sailing through oceans of ink, fighting dragons of doubt, but the pen in my hand is still burning.
Every line I write is a step forward. Every page is a door I'm opening.
And though the road is long, and the critics are loud, I made a promise; I am not throwing away my shot.
For I am Carlie. I am fifteen. And my story is only just beginning.
The world I write is brighter than the world I see.
Because this is my dream. My escape. My story.

And I'll keep dreaming, and dreaming, and dreaming, until all of my dreams become real.
It might take months. It might take years. It might take a lifetime.
But one day, i'li bring those worlds to life.
One word. One page. One brave breath at a time.

Carlie Cassidy (15)

I Thought Martin Luther King Had A Dream

In the heart of humanity's dawn,
Where dreams of equality are born,
Martin's voice rose, clear and bright,
Against the shroud of darkest night.

With courage, he spoke of the day,
When justice would come our way,
When children of every hue,
Would play together, dreams in view.

No more the chains of hate,
No more the walls of fate,
He saw a future, shining bright,
Where love would banish endless night.

Brothers and sisters, black and white,
Hand in hand, we face the fight,
For in unity, we find our might,
To turn the wrongs of past to right.

He dreamed of a table, wide and fair,
Where all are welcome, all have a share,
Where prejudice falls, like dust to the ground,
And the beauty of humanity is finally found.

So let us rise, in his name,
And kindle his eternal flame,
Together, as one, we'll stand tall,
In a world where justice reigns for all.

From every mountain, let freedom ring,
In every heart, let compassion sing,
For in our unity, we see,
The dream of Martin's legacy.

Together, we shall overcome,
And march to the beat of love's own drum,
With every step, every voice, every call,
We'll build a future for us all.

Let us remember, his fight was ours,
To break the chains, to heal the scars,
In unity, we find the key,
To unlock the door to equality.

Brihanna Nsa Inyongo (17)

The Night I Met Myself

Who do you want to be?
That night when I went to sleep,
the only thing on my mind, was the question.
I was standing in a box.
Cold and empty.
Except for the woman in grey.
She was grief-stricken and small.
I said something and she looked up.
Brown eyes she had, and that dark hair.
Those eyes I looked in every day.
They were mine.
She looked briefly confused,
as if some impossible concept
had suddenly come to the surface,
and her mind had tried to grasp it.
Because, that's what I feel.
She cried out, "I failed."
How? I thought, and as if she heard me,
"I can't write, and I'm supposed to be a writer!"
But you can speak, and words that come out of your mouth
are more important than those written on forgettable paper,
"I can hardly speak."
Yet here you are speaking fluent English to me,
which is one of the forgotten wonders of humans,

the art of communication,
"I am a disgraceful representation of us.
I should have never been created."
Silence. She stares. I stare.
I don't care about your mistakes,
I move towards her,
I don't care about your failures,
I touch her hand, because that's who we are,
I touch her fingers to my heart, and we are one.
My heartbeat echoed down around the room.
She smiles, and now I know who I want to be.

Ania Dave (12)

A Have A Dream (To Belong)

I have a dream—not draped in velvet words,
But carved from silence, from glances unheard.
Not a podium cry, not an entire nation's cheer,
But a whisper within: *I just want to be here.*

I dream of a day where my skin's not a code,
Where my voice is not filtered, or softened, or slowed.
Where beauty's not measured by the standards I fear,
And worth isn't tied to the mask that I wear.

I dream of a crowd that sees past the shell,
That knows there's a story I'm aching to tell.
A room I can enter and breathe like I should,
Where I'm not misunderstood for wanting the good.

I dream of a mirror that smiles back at me,
Without saying, "You'd be more loved if you'd just be
A little more this, or a little less that—
Fix your voice, fix your laugh, fix your skin, hide your soul under hats."

I dream of a place that doesn't demand
I shrink or perform just to take someone's hand.
Where 'fitting in' isn't cutting off parts,
But growing into the shape of brave hearts.

Where fashion and filters don't govern my grace,
Where tears on my cheeks aren't reasons for shame.
Where 'weird' becomes wonder, and 'loud' becomes light,
And 'different' is dazzling and perfectly right.

Alaana Bojan (12)

The Cartography Of Skin

I dream of a world where mirrors forget how to wound,
Where their glass no longer slices us into 'too much' and 'not enough',
Where our reflections are not verdicts,
But gentle affirmations of love.

I dream of bodies unlearning their shame,
Of daughters who never count calories like sins,
Of sons who know softness is not a flaw,
Of every soul allowed to exist without apology.

I dream of a future where beauty is not a cage,
But a language, a language spoken in scars and wrinkles,
In birthmarks and silver hairs,
Across the sacred map of a body that chose to stay alive.

I dream of generations raised on different stories,
Of children who inherit mirrors that speak kindly,
Of teenagers who trace their reflections with wonder,
Of adults who then grow to understand that 'being' was always enough,
Of the elderly who can look back and admire their life, not regret.

I dream of humans to be like nature,
How? Well, because the sky does not edit its clouds,
Oceans do not shame their waves,
And mountains do not beg to be smaller.

I dream of a day when mirrors become windows,
Where we look in and see not flaws, but futures,
Each freckle a story, each curve a chapter,

And every breath a vow, that we are our own hereafter.

Maram Abukar (16)

To Be Proud Of My Voice

I come from a place full of vitriol and hate. We pretend to have moved on, to be equals and not afraid, but I see and hear the way we act. The way we point fingers and mutter under our breaths. I see the divides, clear as days, even on a simple walk through town.

Picture a road. It's not a bad road; the paint is worn off, yes, but it's fairly smooth. It's usable. It is framed, on either side, by two big walls. They each depict a flag. Royal blue and rural green. Flags should be symbols of pride, of patriotism but in my eyes, it is a symbol of war. You drive between two solid walls, standing off against each other, and feel overwhelmingly trapped.

I feel no pride. I have never felt an ounce of pride in my life. I have felt tearing, gut-destroying shame at the flicker of fire, or the spitting of cruel words, but never pride.

Except for when I write.

I'm not very good at it. I can't even format a poem. I know few rhyming words or when to split my lines. I know not of sonnets or pentameters, but I know of the guttural urge to speak. To voice my mind, share something deep inside, and feel the faintest ghost of pride touch upon my words.

I dream, each night, of escaping this small town. Of licking, just about tasting, something akin to pride. Of being heard.

I have a dream. And so, I write.

Olive Shaw (16)

Hands That Heal

I have a dream,
Not of crowns or riches,
But of hands that heal,
Of footsteps moving quietly through bright halls,
Carrying hope where silence hurts.

I dream of a world
Where suffering finds an answer,
Where shaking hands find comfort
In the calm of my voice,
Where pain is not a prison
But a doorway to light.

I see myself standing close to life's edge,
A keeper of breath,
A builder of second chances,
Mending the broken with knowledge,
And lifting the weary with kindness.

I dream of charts filled not just with numbers,
But with names,
Each one a story worth holding,
Each heartbeat a reminder
That healing is not only science,
It is compassion in action.

I dream of learning the language of the body,
The rhythm of veins,
The music hidden in every heartbeat,
Turning knowledge into comfort,
And study into care.

Yes, I have a dream:
To build bridges between despair and hope,
To walk into the night with a light in my hands,
To serve, to guide, to heal.

And though the road is long,
With heavy books and sleepless nights,
I will keep going,
Because my dream is not just mine,
But a promise to the world
That I will stand strong
Where healing is needed most.

Aadrika Singh (15)

Change

I dream of something that borders perfection.
Not a distant planet or luxury lifestyle,
But for the world's attitude to change its direction,
To become a place which nurtures difference.

I dream of change.
Right now, unresolved cries for help are being shushed,
Their owners feel abnormally out of place.
Especially at school where they're picked at and pushed
Until marginalised tears run hot down their face.

I dream of change.
There's that boy I know, who avoids his own image,
He's convinced his character is too much to bear.
His drained eyes whisper of the love he longs for but can never have,
So his heart holds onto the words which he knows can't be shared.

Change begins to flicker.
They're aware their community is silently slipping,
It threatens to erase itself from history.
People are dying, they're mistreated and unheard.
No one makes time to hear their stories.

Change is fading.
So there you sit.
You hope for the fixing generation to solve all your issues.

Maybe that time would come quicker if they weren't forced to be invisible.
Yet, since they are just that, they lie, surrounded by sodden tissues,
Stripped of the chance to live a life of liberty.

Change is impossible.

Reece Oakley (15)

Academic Desires

Primary was a blast, learning about the past,
respect all the casts in our plays throughout all the days.
The years have gone so fast,
the journey from Year Five to Six gave off some vibes,
but now it's time to focus, SATS are coming up,
learning, learning, learning, never giving up,
there were times of boredom and times of fun,
but we kept on going, crushing our tests,
Mr and Ms never ever failing to help us obtain
the maximum knowledge to upgrade our brains,
it's coming to the end, we must comprehend,
goodbye primary school, we are all contrite,
remember, we are all humans, it's time to unite!
Things are going smoothly, we're missing our friends,
but as I said, we must comprehend,
it's just a part of life, if we don't move on, we will fall behind.
Thank the Lord for giving us education
and keeping us from starvation,
we shall thrive as a nation
and make the world a better place through education.
I have a dream, a dream to inspire,
bringing people's days from lower to higher.
I want to be truthful, no longer a liar.
Year Seven is a spark, igniting my fire,

if I do good, I get the life I desire.
It's not too late to ignite your fire.
It's now or never, chase your desires.

Kario Medford (12)

Our Lost Vows

I want to unlearn him.
I want to unlearn the feeling of his arms around my neck,
the imprint of his smile against my eyelids,
the pitch of his voice when he'd whisper into my ear.
But every time I try to,
I am reminded of the treacherous beauty of us.

Even now, I can still feel his voice echoing around me,
it consumes me until I'm swimming
in an unwelcome sense of familiarity
and makes me jump out of fear of sinking into old habits.
I am now alone in this life:
his absence a catalyst for disaster
as I realise that I'm a puzzle piece in the wrong picture.

Despite never projecting the three-word oath,
I know we both swore to it...
It's something I'll never be capable of breaking,
so I keep a fragment of him beside me,
silent, for as long as I'll live
and visit him personally during my nightly dances
with Death, where I'll meet him next.

Among the amenities of the alternate world,
would our unspoken promise slip his mind?
I fear that he'll reduce me to nothing but a memory,

knowing fully well that our bond remains to be my sword,
my sanctuary.
Or he may be watching my every move,
possibly with somebody new,
critiquing or caring, I'll never know.

Riyah Imaan (17)

A Dream Through The Window

I walk across a dark hallway,
It finds me,
I stare through the window,
Across the world my eyes have yet to see.

How can this be so picture-perfect?
Everything feels so correct.
Children's smiles light up the sky,
People's spirits rising high.

No more invisible walls,
Now every heart meets all.
Every book, every cover, and all in between,
Becomes the heart for each other, in a world of green.

Green—green is the colour of the lungs,
While every soul sings the same song,
In tune with the bees and other kinds,
A march where no one is left behind.

Freedom is printed like a tattoo,
With all the pain they've been through.
But justice is what they hold,
A world so brave and bold.

Rustle, wake—I open my eyes to a blank ceiling,
Moments ago, I was in that longing feeling.

I walk across my room, once a dark hallway,
On the ground I've always been on, every day.

I stare through the window, into the cold December,
Gold shines through the night sky like a glowing ember.
A silent thunder rumbles in my heart,
From my dream I see my spark,
A trace of a new aspiration to start,
All it takes is as little as a dream.

Thasara Wijenayaka Kankanamge (13)

The Dreams I Wish I Knew

Being young and cheerful,
I had a lot of joy,
emotions I wanted to share with others, things I wanted to express.
And so I wrote,
I wanted to be an author,
an artist who illustrates their own books, their own poems and their own words.
I'd followed that dream,
Yet the absence of my father lingered in my mind.
The feeling of grief knowing he was somewhere,
Often he was mentally present,
Yet I felt the pain - the wrath,
I attempted to study psychology,
Knowing all of these new feelings,
all of these new ways to feel,
I struggled to continue—my heart was empty.
My grades failed,
my dreams slowly fade into the alluring abyss,
I fell into a dark, scary place.
I can't focus,
I can't move,
I am a figure—broken and frail.
My dreams seep through,
and so I write,
those feelings pass through,

I wanted to write so everyone could feel,
so I could express my pain and anguish.
so you could understand why I felt the way I do.
but nothing feels the same, I'm stuck - as I've always been.
My dreams seem false,
they seem young and unachievable,
I am unknown to my dream.

I wish I knew what dream I sought.

Italy-Faith Fox (16)

The Cartography Of Me

There's a woman I wish I'd met
A woman I'd like you to meet
With lived skin carved of sandalwood, and two blue snifters of the Nile
She tells a story, not with ink, but with scar, wrinkle, and smile
You point at her nose, squint at its asymmetry
The woman winks, "Haven't you seen the opera house of Sydney?"
You sneer at her thighs as she doesn't walk; she strides
She tells you the columns of Parthenon strengthen and stabilise
You stare at her stretch marks as she reclines in her chair
She asks if you've ever grown another human in there
Resilience of skin and wit of tongue
Force of gaze and vigour of lung
Colour
Pulse
Drive and bite
Touch, will, smirk, and might
Not a noun, not a pretty thing
Alive. Moving. Tingling
She can't be condensed to fit on a scale, powdered and preened into a hashtagged fairy tale
By the power of her arms and the point of her toe
My body does not feel to not ache, tremble and glow
It does not heal to not fall, to grow and not give it my all

And at last when I'm done
When I'm finally done
I'll go dancing and singing
Ignorant of 'she'
Because I found home
In me.

Kirstin Thomson (16)

Celestial Pursuit

I have this recurring whimsical dream:

When my hand grasps the slumber of dreamlight,
My blanket unravels to quaint, starry silver threads,
The warmth of its mellow embrace evaporates like mist in starlight,
And rather a gold sea of seamless stars becomes my bed.

My soft pillow retreats and floats away from beneath my head,
Carried away by cosmic messengers towards the silent moon,
It retreats from me, leaving a silvery trail ahead,
I solely chase its shimmering path to where the cosmos bloom.

My eager ears attend to the celestial night's soft tune,
My reflective eyes fixated on the enchanting galaxies,
My inquisitive hands stretch above for the glittering moon,
My thoughts scattered within their radiant fantasies.

Then, my sight lies upon the planets that sway ever so carefully,
Like astronomic dancers in a cosmic trance,
The Sun and Moon exchange harmony tenderly,
Conducting the sky's eternal dance.

Soon, the fragile dream dissolves and the captivating visions flee,
The silver threads of my wistful blanket weave back instead,
I still fondly reminisce about that shimmering silver path, beckoning me,
Which lingers as a twinkle in my restless mind and glowing bed.

I awaken, contemplate and softly think to myself,
Perhaps my place is somewhere among the stars.

Sia Kumar (15)

The Battle Between

I am torn between two worlds,
Torn between the bleeding sunset,
Behind the Tyne Bridge,
And the spicy crackle of samosas,
Wafting across the bazaar's warm haze.
Attachment cannot be dissolved,
Just like how,
The frost on our car refused to melt,
On the chilly mornings before school,
And how even the most grievous of fights,
Could not shatter the bonds between family.
My trials may not be a tempest,
Aired for all to witness,
But there is a hurricane rippling beneath my ribs,
Tearing at my heart,
Cleaving at my soul.
As I sever tangled roots,
With my glowing sword of heartbreak,
And plant new seeds,
In strangely familiar soil.
As I distance from pain,
Only to find,
My careful stitches snagged,
On the jagged shards of memory.
I belong to nowhere, and to everywhere,
I belong with my family, but still alone,

I belong to my home, but live in its exile.
Forever destined,
To watch beauty from a distance,
To admire the lives I revelled in,
Never to enter either again.
Through sickness,
And health,
Through trials
And tribulations.
Through every entrance,
And into,
My final,
Exile.

Abiha Khurram (15)

I Still Dream

I have a dream that social media won't steal my peace,
that I won't measure myself by likes and comments,
that school won't crush me with pressure until I can't even breathe.
I have a dream that the Earth won't keep dying while people scroll past it,
that oceans won't choke on plastic,
that trees won't fall for greed.
I have a dream that being a black girl won't mean being called 'loud',
won't mean being labelled 'sassy',
won't mean being told to sit down when I was born to stand tall.
I have a dream that slavery won't be brushed over like it's embarrassing,
that teachers won't speak it soft,
that when they do, I don't feel the whole class staring at me,
like I'm the history, not the student.
I have a dream that black history is not just October,
not just a side note, but the truth we carry every day.
I have a dream that the justice system isn't just another word for injustice,
that racist minds don't get to write the laws.
I have a dream today.

And even with fear, even with hate, even with pain,
I still dream,
because dreaming is power, and I refuse to let it go.

Favour Sulahiman (13)

My Dream Maker

The bell's harsh clang, a year begun,
With minds so sharp, yet still undone.
KS4, the age of fire,
Where futures form, or aspirations tire.

A syllabus, a mountain high,
With prose and verse beneath the sky.
We climb, we teach, with passion's flame,
Igniting sparks, to whisper a name.

For in these rooms, where theories bloom,
And exam papers loom,
We see the doubt, the hidden fear,
The whispered, "Can I?" from the anxious ear.

We sculpt with words, a sculptor's art,
Each lesson etched upon the heart.
A poem's power, a formula's might,
To guide them toward their own clear light.

We watch them wrestle, learn, and strive,
To keep their dreams and hopes alive.
Then, slowly, through the blur of stress,
A confidence begins to express.

A pupil's question, sharp and new,
A thoughtful answer, brave and true.

These are the moments, pure and bright,
That make the endless struggle right.

For in this crucible, strong and deep,
Where futures are in trust to keep,
We forge the leaders, wise and kind,
And leave our own bright spark behind.

Scarlet Elton (12)

What I See

I hope he falls for my eyes
And doesn't let his drift from mine,
I hope his gaze doesn't fall below my shoulders
Scanning every part of me I wish were hidden
Because as soon as he catches glimpse of my body
He'll see what I see.
It won't be love in his eyes, instead they'll reflect mine.

I hope he falls for my heart
Ignoring what contains it, how it longs for a type of love it has never received,
I hope he'll never look at my waist, chest, or legs
Because I don't want him to see what I see.

I hope he falls for my mind
And how it works and strives, not what gnaws
At my thoughts when I'm alone.
Although my mind betrays, lingering on unimportance
For so long, I'd prefer him focus on that, rather than
The things I'm focusing on.

I hope he falls for me, although he never will
My mind keeps hoping
Pleading him to ignore what I see,
If he did, my eyes, my heart, my mind
Wouldn't matter.
Only the unfitting skin covering everything I hate.

I don't want him to see me, I realise
Because I don't like what I see, so
Why would he?

Diana Mota (15)

Scream And Shout

I could shout and I could scream,
and you would know just what I mean,
if you were willing to lend an ear,
and actually listen and actually hear.

Because it doesn't matter how I grew up,
at some point, we all have to grow up,
and you have lived longer than I,
but I have more to fear and more reason to cry.

To cry out to the people who grow up beside me,
to those who believe they've grown up already,
to shout out the things that I believe in,
so others can find their own voice from within.

I do it because I know that I'm able,
to speak up for those with no seat at this table,
because we are running out of places to sit,
it's becoming so common for voices to quit,

but there are so many conflicts that need to be won,
and you cannot quit something that hasn't begun,
maybe these battles do not even need to start,
but preventing them is an unmastered art.

So for those who have never had their own choice,
scream and shout out if you have the voice,
to share so many viewpoints and every uniqueness,
because having a dream is never a weakness.

Mia Young (16)

Dreams Are...

Dreams are such strange things,
They lie, they deceive, they tell you what you want most in the world.
And then you wake up.

Dreams are such cruel things,
They plague your every thought, you have no choice over what you think, what you think about every second.
And then they rip it all away.

Dreams are such horrific things,
They would tell you your worst nightmares, whisper dark and demanding words in your brain, they would implant the things you didn't even know you were afraid of,
And then they would make sure you can't escape; they would bind you down.

But dreams... dreams are such sweet things,
They can show you how life would be different, they give you ideas of hope, of life, of joy.
They make sure that you can be who you want to be, say what you want to say, hear all the things you want to hear.
Then... they can take it all away.

But you still have the sweet sounds flickering away in your head.

They sing, they sigh, they scream.
All the things you could be, will circle your mind
Until they can become true.
So, I suppose that I have a dream.

Avneet Pannu (14)

I Once Had A Dream

When I was three my dream was to make hearts for sick people so families didn't have to lose people like I lost my grandad.
At five years old, I wanted to teach children gymnastics.
However, at seven, I wanted to be a singer as I was good.
But enough of that. Let's talk about what I really want. I dream for all war to be stopped because it's childish. What do you mean two countries fought because of selfishness and greed for more land?
I also dream for a cure for everything. So many people have lost family. So many children born with incurable diseases and not being able to live a life without hospitalisation or treatment.
But most importantly, I dream of fairness around the world. Not a world where people feel left out or worthless, just one where they feel valued and appreciated by everyone, no matter what colour skin they have, what their religion is or who their family are. These things are something you can't do anything about.
These are my dreams. Though they might seem impossible to do, every idea, every project or even life-changing decision all starts with a dream.

Natalie Wojcik (12)

Because You Wouldn't Tell It

She was swallowed by unbecoming, peeling the rind from her own name, hanging it beside the wasp-nests in the attic where old selves hum like mourning
She wrote in ash
In the aftermath of the forgotten
Her hands, burnt maps, each finger a compass bent toward somewhere she'd never lived
What is it to wish and wish and wish?
To stand still while her town swelled like a bruise?
So she fed the silence its own tongue
And slept in dresses stitched from frost
They told her not to speak unless you bloom
But the garden was growing twisted tongues
And the mirror only ever showed a girl mid-molt, all bone and apology
Still she learned to birth the fire, not bury it
She trained herself to split the sky open like a pomegranate, letting every seed fall and rot into something radiant into the hands who reach for them
This is no anthem. It's her whisper I speak of, dug from under the floorboards, a ghost learning to pronounce her name
She had a dream, we found it washed up ashore, kissed by the sand
And sailed away with it in my writing.

Amira Cheung Simhani (14)

I Have A Dream

I have a dream,
That silence will no longer be the language of the unheard,
That voices will rise like dawn over valleys of doubt,
And truth will walk freely, unchained by fear.

I have a dream,
That kindness will not be a currency spent in scarcity,
But a flood that drowns hatred in its wake,
That children will grow up knowing peace not as a stranger,
But as a neighbour who never leaves.

I have a dream,
That borders will be bridges, not walls,
That difference will be a dance, not a divide,
And no one will be judged by the scars they carry,
But by the light they choose to shine.

I have a dream,
That the tired will rest, the hungry will eat,
The lonely will be seen, and the broken will be whole.
That hope will not be a whisper,
But a roar that shakes the foundations of despair.

I have a dream,
And though the road is long and the night is deep,
I will walk it with faith, with fire, with love,
Because dreams are not just for sleeping.
They are for waking the world.

Tamsyn Skehan (13)

A Difference Begins With Me

I whispered to the world, "Don't cry."
Her rivers trembled, her forests sighed.
She answered softly, "Child, be strong,
One voice can grow a thousand songs."

I walk through the streets of stone and steel,
Where hurried hearts forget to feel.
Yet hope still flickers, bright and small,
A candle's glow can light it all.

I plant a seed in broken ground,
Its roots reach deep, its leaves reach round.
The soil hums love, the sunlight sings,
The breeze repeats: 'Change starts with wings.'

I am a drop in the restless sea,
But waves are born from drops like me.
Like thunder rolling, loud and free,
Together we shape destiny.

I dream of skies where people can soar,
Of open hands, not fists of war.
The world is weary, scarred, yet true,
She waits for me, she waits for you.

So step by step, we'll mend her scars,
We'll light the night with blazing stars.
Remember this, let voices rise:
The smallest spark can paint the skies.

Harriet Saunders (12)

O'Aqsa, We Will Not Forget

Beneath the broken sky, they kneel,
Where grief is sharp, and wounds don't heal.
Masjid Al-Aqsa, sacred light,
Now weeps beneath the dead of night.

Its walls have heard the Prophet's tread,
Now echo cries for those who bled.
A mother holds her child and prays,
Their world in ruins, faith still stays.

To us, it's more than stone and dome,
It is our heart, our soul, our home.
O Ummah, hear the call, the pain,
Their tears fall soft like mercy's rain.

Shall we be silent while they bleed,
Ignore the orphan's cry, the need?
Or rise as one—in Dua, in Deed,
Planting strength where tyrants feed.

For Al-Aqsa's flame is not yet gone,
It burns in hearts that carry on.
Through shattered stone and darkened skies,
The prayer of truth will always rise.

We see. We stand. We're near.
From every land, from every tongue,
We raise the cry of old and young,
Until the chains are all undone,
And justice shines beneath the sun.

Rayyan Piper (14)

Tomorrow Is Yesterday's Paradox

I wanted to capture the beauty of Mother Nature.
Or record myself preaching to the birds that would listen.
But blood that rushes through pulsates a signal to be a lifeline for others,
Yet the black holes puncturing the source suck out all that golden blood.
Both fighting to either help others or vexed with the thought of people who know less.
To help others love but wince when others act weird.
But what I need is to know me.
A sea of hands push and shove, screeching commands, but do I want this.
I feel like a ghost ship in the middle of a vast sea, no map or compass to be a guide, or a rope being dragged from both sides.
Is this a team effort or do I have to add the I in team?
All the time chasing others' acceptance is looked upon highly like golden blood.
But am I like golden blood?
I dream of peeling back the layers of my life, to find the core.
The surface hasn't been scratched yet.
I yearn to know me, but is that too eager?
I beg, but that's too much.
This dream is lucid, my blood is red.

Ellvina De-Graft Jordan (12)

Flight

My dreams are pretty weird
That's to say the least
Sometimes they range from finding dead relatives
To obtaining world peace
But there's one I cherish
One that appears every night
A dream reality where I can finally leave the ground
And take flight, I fly over my family,
They smile as they see me soar
No matter how many times I see the ground like this I never get bored
The floor is green, to say the least
Garbage gone, and everyone is able to feast
There'd be no anger, no fights,
There'd be kids outside on the streets flying brand new kites
The children's devices would be boring
And all the kids would be playing, even when the rain is pouring
No wars, famine or loss.
This is the society I want, no matter the cost
But even when I wake up, tangled in my sheets
I think it might be possible, if everyone these days didn't care about stupid tweets
Get off your phones and go outside
The worst you can say is that I didn't even try.

Tiana Radder (17)

I Have A Dream (That Homework Disappeared)

I have a dream - not wild, but bold,
Of freedom from worksheets, tired and old.
No more maths at midnight, eyes half-shut,
No more essays with coffee in my gut.

I dream of backpacks light as air,
Of evenings free from teacher's glare.
Where weekends bloom with time to play,
And Mondays don't steal joy away.

I dream of learning that feels alive,
Of building rockets that actually drive.
Of painting planets, coding games,
Not ticking boxes, chasing grades.

I dream of questions that spark a fire,
Of lessons shaped by real desire.
Where curiosity leads the way,
And homework simply fades away.

I dream of teachers who say, "Explore!"
Not, "Finish page 94."
Of classrooms buzzing, minds set free,
Of learning that feels like being me.

I have a dream - it's loud, it's clear,
A world where homework disappears.
Where kids can breathe, create, and roam,
And school feels just like coming home.

Julian Mbalisike (13)

Quiet(!) Kid

The quiet kid sat steadfast, silent, just listening and watching and waiting for the next shower of shells. Some days the drizzle could be whipped off, leaving a damp uniform. Other days, gunshot wounds would turn storm clouds red and the quiet kid would drown. *What was so bad about being quiet?* the quiet kid used to wonder, *couldn't we just live in peace?*

Months later, the quiet kid had had enough and struck back. They never cared until the quiet kid started to react. An unarmed, unwanted monster amongst a battlefield of righteous men. "This is unacceptable behaviour," the commander screamed, forcing a white flag into the quiet monster's claws.

No... NO! It won't end like this! I refuse. This is my story, and I'll be the one to write it for the Quiet Kid who needed to hear it. For the 'monsters' unheard. For the forced sacrifices. With this pen in my battered hand, true peace I'll demand. So no quiet kid has to drown or fight again. For my dream is for the world to put love first.

Kristopher Robin Perseus Beasley (17)

A Beautiful Town

Bursting with fountains of radiance in the town square,
fluorescent flowers bloom gracefully everywhere.
The gentle flow of the glassy river
makes people who row gasp and shiver.
Bustling shops and walkways, so pretty,
are home to animals that are the most witty.
Dense trees and lush, velvety carpets of green
dress the town in robes of shimmering turquoise sheen.
Pristine swimming pools, adorned with hot tubs,
shine brighter with pool lights resembling neighbouring clubs.
Rose gold hues of the rising sun
dance upon early-wakers having lots of fun.
Cyclists and pedestrians chuckling amongst themselves
match words written in a book on some library shelves.
Yoga meditators stretching in open, water-viewed glass domes
make videos to go viral and enjoy in their homes.
School children who race home after school
daydream about vivid moments of play, which they think are cool.
A beautiful town glows and shines in glory
like mythical towns in wonderful stories.

Shanaya Koul (12)

Dangerous Love

Today, tomorrow, forever

I hate you
I love you
I want you
two minds intertwine
but why mine?
our eyes interlock
and just like that, time stops
I hate you, I love you, I want you
I'm crazy, going out of my mind, our souls they bind
and I am blind
my mind says no but my heart screams yes
a dangerous pull I cannot confess
every touch burns, every silence screams
we are prisoners caught in forbidden dreams
but to turn away means to tear us apart
but why stay just for you to break my heart?
I love you
I hate you
I want you
I am yours and you are mine
but I hear you whisper every line
so are you really mine or am I just yours?
drowning, now pulled ashore
I chase the night, you haunt the day

your kiss is poison, it's breaking me away
within each day I fade away
if love is fate then let ours break
if our love is a risk, it's the one I'll take

today, tomorrow, forever.

Eva Keegan (12)

Unsealed

Twisting the lid with steady hands,
Glass-sun-warmed, and old.
The threads resist, like time itself,
Guarding truths untold.
The glass is clear, the seal is tight,
Yet I have learned to stand and fight.
Beyond this small, unyielding jar,
Justice hides in shadows, far.
But in my mind, I wear the robe,
The courtroom hush, the weight I hold.
Truth and law within my clasp,
A dream long chased through bitten lips.
Then—pop! A breath, a gasp of air,
The jar rolls free—my soul laid bare.
And there she sits—my younger self,
Cross-legged, clutching a stubborn book.
She never spoke, but oh, she heard;
Every wound became a word.
Now grown, I rise, my voice a flame,
Not for glory, not for fame,
But for the child whose hope decays.
The jar sits silent on the shelf,
Yet it unlocked my truest self.
A vessel small, yet vast inside,
A weight, a key, my guiding light.
To justice. To rebirth. To dignity.

Sarah-Mariah Sebastian (13)

The Dream That Stands For All

I have a dream—not just for me,
But for a world where everyone is free.
Where no one's judged by skin or name,
And love and justice burn the same.
Where borders bend to open hands,
And every culture proudly stands.
Where girls can lead, and boys can cry,
And truth is never told a lie.
I dream of classrooms loud with hope,
Not silence caused by lack of scope.
Where children rise, no matter race,
To find their power—claim their place.
Where wealth is not the gate to worth,
And peace is planted in the earth.
Where who you love won't bring you shame,
And all are called by their true name.
Where wheels or walkers don't define,
The dreams we chase, the heights we climb.
Where labels break, and we begin
To see the light beneath the skin.
I dream of leaders brave and kind,
Of open hearts and open minds.
A world where all can proudly say,
"I matter here—I lead the way."

Aleeza Hussain (12)

To Teach

Ever since I was a little girl,
I always wanted to be a teacher,
Teaching my stuffed animals,
Taking the register of an imaginary class,
Even printing out work for my teddies.
I want to care,
To help,
To be the favourite teacher,
I know how tough school is.
I joined high school and when I was bullied,
A teacher helped me,
I want to be like her,
I see how unfairly kids are treated,
If you are naughty, you get a reward,
If you behave, you get nothing,
I want to change that.
I want to help people,
I want to be there, to care,
I want to be the teacher kids come to when upset,
Or if they don't understand.
If a teacher isn't listening, I will,
Being bullied and nothing is getting done?
I want to be able to help.
I'm working hard to achieve my dream,

I hope I can make a change in someone's life,
I have a dream to be a history teacher,
To care, to help and to be there for support.

Olivia Smith (15)

To Be RICH

I have a dream:
to be RICH,
not just in money,
but in the kind of person I am.

R–Respectful
I want to be respectful,
to treat everyone kindly,
and to always stay humble,
even when I achieve big things.

I–Intelligent
I want to be smart,
to learn and grow,
to make good choices,
and to follow my dreams.

C–Caring
I want to be caring,
to help people when I can,
and to make the world a little better
by being kind.

H–Happy
I want a happy life,
a loving family,
friends who smile with me,
and a home full of laughter.

I want my name to be spoken with pride
by my family,
because they see what I worked for.

Being RICH is more than money or success:
it's about respect, intelligence, care, and happiness.
It's about living the life I dream of
and becoming the person I want to be.

Macy Miller (13)

Do You Dream Too?

I have a dream, both bright and true,
Of skies of hope, for me and you.
Where every voice is free to sing.
And joy can rise on freedom's wing.

I dream of hands of every hue,
Joined together, strong and true.
Of bridges built, not walls of stone,
A world where none must stand alone.

I dream of classrooms filled with light,
Where every child's future is bright.
Where books are doors and dreams take flight,
And wrong is challenged by the right.

I dream of hearts that choose to care,
Of kindness spreading everywhere.
Of courage rising when times are tough,
And knowing love is strong enough.

I dream of peace that will not fade,
Of promises of justice made.
Where rivers flow through fields of green,
And all are valued, heard, and seen.

I have a dream, do you dream too?
A world remade, both fair and new.
Where what we wish is what we see,
And all of us can live as we.

Ibrahim Qureshi (13)

The Dream That Waits

I have a dream, it waits and it sleeps
until the day I can reach out and leap.
I have a dream of a bright light
on a stage in the night,
a crowd in awe,
lending their applause.
I have a dream of a world where every voice is heard,
where dangers are seen, and compassion is heard.
I have a dream of a classroom brimming with curious hearts,
yearning for knowledge and brighter tomorrows.
I have a dream I may never see,
a world of kindness and a quiet peace,
where the Earth is free, unburdened by our survival.
I have a dream where we live in harmony,
no fear, no misery.
A world of hope and love,
where we live as pure as the flight of a dove.
I have a dream, it waits and it sleeps
until the day I can reach out and leap,
with ambitions that burn like gold,
no longer young, unsure of what I'm told,
wanting a future, bright and true,
filled with joy and peace.
And a dawn, where the Earth breathes free.

Shaye Kelly (15)

The Grading Game

The morning bell screams, I drag through the door,
lockers all slamming, my feet on the floor.
The teacher is talking, the clock ticks slow,
I'm writing down notes I don't even know.

They tell me to focus, they tell me 'behave',
but I'm not a robot, I'm not a slave.
They measure my worth by the grades I bring,
as if letters on paper define everything.

I study for hours, my eyes turn sore,
yet the test still says I should try more.
The smartest kids get the gold star prize,
while effort like mine goes unseen, despised.

I'm told I'll fail if I don't comply,
but they don't see how hard I try.
I'm more than a score, more than a grade,
but none of that counts in the system they've made.

So I sit in silence, play my part,
but it eats away at a tired heart.
Because school's supposed to help me grow,
yet all it does is tell me 'no'.

Niamh Robinson (13)

Chains I Cannot See

I have a voice,
but sometimes it feels small,
whispering against the roar of silence,
that hides behind closed doors.

I see faces,
young eyes dimmed by fear,
dreams stolen before they could bloom;
hands tied by invisible chains.

I dream I could reach through the darkness,
grab those lost souls,
and pull them back into the light:
where freedom breathes.

I carry their stories in my chest,
the silent screams, the shattered hopes,
and I want to shout:
to break the walls,
to tear the shadows away.

I dream of a world where no one is a secret,
where every child, every woman, every man
walks unchained, unafraid:
where love is stronger than the greed that steals lives.

I am not powerless,
because in every heartbeat,

there's a fight, a promise,

to see, to speak, to stop,

until the chains are gone,
and all are free to dream again.

Emilia Sirbu (15)

Invisible... Until One Day

I sit in class, my pen still,
my eyes on the board
but my mind replaying last night.
Hours. Hours cutting, trimming, shaping,
every second of my video
stitched together with my heart.
And when I pressed upload, I prayed.
I prayed for someone to notice.
But the likes never came.
The silence swallowed me whole.
It feels like the teacher here,
voice cracking with exhaustion,
marking piles of books until midnight;
so much love, so much effort,
only for the world to shrug and move on.
And here I sit, wondering if I'm the same.
If my dream is nothing but wasted breath,
a star I'll never touch.
But somewhere beneath the ache,
a spark fights to live.
A voice whispering,
"One day, they will see you.
One day, they will know you mattered."
So, I hold on.

Because even if I am only a whisper today,
I have a dream to one day
become the song the world cannot forget.

Riya Maniz Carsane (16)

Dazzling Dreams

I dream I'm running through a fair,
Stalls filled with clocks and sand.
The jesters hum beneath the stair,
They laugh, fist-bumping me by the hand!
I dream I'm climbing through a light,
Each step a colour I cannot name.
The air, too thick—but just about right!
Then someone calls me from the flame.
Tessellation spins round my head,
A vault of moving marquetry.
Each and every panel with threads of lead,
Folding themselves around a key! Blimey!
They shimmer, they twist, they reappear,
These ideas coming with no plan.
Each dream, a universe bright and clear,
Unfolding faster than I can!
I dream I'm shrinking as I sprint,
The floor, growing underneath my feet.
A tower built with sweet, sweet mint,
Falls happily into the heat.
A funfair I see across the horizon,
Buzzing with joy and a beautiful band...
Cheerful tunes and music flies in.
Indescribable! Dreams are never bland!

Marvin Selasie Diameh Acquah (12)

In My Own World...

My eyes flutter shut and my mind takes me away,
away from the corrupt, away from myself, a paradise I can stay.
I dream up a world of my own, sun, magic and stars,
these colourful ideas piled up on a throne, the flicker of candlelight, the hope, like Earth to Mars.
It's never night, only ever bright, the sun casting shapes against my shut eyes,
the warmth bathing my skin, no one to hear my cries.
A place of my own, yet that feeling still nags.
It pulls at my heart, a devotion tags.
A craving to be seen,
to be held and cherished, not through a useless screen.
I have a dream where I'm not separating the sweetness from reality,
but seeing the two as a combined duality.
That when I open my eyes, colour still stays,
compassion ablaze,
at the core of my writing,
lingering in the back of my mind like flickering lightning.
That dream burns at my beating heart, searing a hole through my chest,
the emptiness blessed.

Emily Sawyer (15)

The Life I Yearn For

I wake up every day thinking how many problems I'll have to face,
Homework, chores, feeling my life is out of place.
Wanting to achieve, to become someone, make my parents proud,
Yet I'm stuck being too young to share my opinions aloud.
Getting told to live in the moment, "Have fun," they say,
But I have to start now, if I want to be successful someday.
My heart wants something greater, I won't let this go,
These elephantine dreams, when time moves so slow.
Suddenly, I'm in court! Dressed in formal attire,
I speak with intention, words like bullets that I fire.
Defending what I believe, fighting for justice and I win!
Yet I wake up again thinking, *when will this life begin?*
Once again, I face the new day, with my mind set,
Daydreaming constantly, even for a second I won't forget.
I clean my room, do the laundry, vacuum the floor,
I just can't help but want something more.

Julia Wozniak (14)

Dreams

Apparently, or well so I'm told, dreams have meanings,
But I'm not sure I'm sold,
Because unless a dream about a broccoli dog,
Or a scary cupboard monster,
Or a really big frog,
Have meanings about how my life will turn out,
Then I'm not sure I believe it,
I have a bit of doubt,
Although there was that one night when I dreamed about chips,
And the next day we got a takeaway,
So maybe I believe it a bit,
But not much though 'cause that can't be true,
Because I recently found out it's thoughts leaving your head,
Who knew? Apparently, some scientists,
But then last week I dreamt about a spider on Mars,
But the closest thing I'd thought about that day was a vase,
But you do have to say it would look good in that empty spot full of flowers, My mind is going too fast now, it's all a blur,
Maybe I'll go have a dream,
My imagination can take it from there.

Lucy Crompton (14)

The Dream I Carry

Since I was young, I've carried a wish,
To guide small hearts as they grow strong,
To watch their kind soul help others out,
To help them flourish and watch them grow old,

I won't just be a teacher,
I'll be their family guiding them through life,
They won't just be cared for,
They will be loved like my own,

Although I will not be their mother,
I will guide them through life,
I will see every accomplishment,
And help them to achieve their goals,

I will understand their language,
And listen with concern,
They can come to me for comfort,
And they will leave with nothing but happiness,

They will proudly show their work to me,
I will respond with the proudest cheers,
No, I'm not their mother,
But my role is just as strong,

So I will follow my dreams,
In hopes I will succeed,
To help those children be their very best.

Lilly May Brennan (14)

I Had A Dream

I had a dream
I stood in front of their faces
The same ones who told me I wouldn't go places
In my doctor's coat I stood proud
I didn't boast or scream but my success spoke loud

I had a dream
Of living in the country I've wanted to since I was a child
But they told me it was too hard, that my dream was too wild
I sat there in the expensive country in a mansion that belonged to me
Those who said it was too expensive and impossible could now see

I had a dream
Of a world full of peace
Where war and genocide are at cease
Unity of different race and religion filling the air
People's hearts filled with kindness, respect, love and care

I lived a dream
Even though people put me down
They said I wouldn't be able to leave this town

I lived a dream
Because I took an act
On what I believed was a fact.

Aimal Waqas (13)

Wonderful World

Run the world and make it wonderful.
Be brave! Be ambitious. Rule the world!
Make the world wonderful.
Make the world a better place.
Be kind. Be happy. Live and laugh.
Make the world wonderful.
Let plants grow and bloom.
Let plants thrive and flourish.
No more littering.
Make the planet a clean and tidy place.
Be proud and protect our planet.
Never give up on your dreams.
Never give up on your hopes and dreams for the future.
Let your hopes and dreams come true!

W onderful world.
O rganise. Be organised.
N ever give up.
D etermination.
E nthusiasm.
R ule the world.
F un.
U nique.
L earning.

W ork and discover.
O pportunities.
R espect and research.
L aughter makes the world a happier place.
D aydream and let your dreams come true!

Jennifer Nile (18)

Crack A Smile

Oh, what fun would it be to be a director
A passionate film creator
The thrill of bringing a set to life submerges me
Helping people with big dreams feel
Let them feel the joy of entertaining people
The elderly in nursing homes
To the children playing with their teddies and dolls
Should have a chance to laugh and cry
To help hospitalised kids have hope in their veins
Let people in depression smile
Actors come from small places and then leave happy
Actresses come and they go
Yet they never leave that pride that courses through
When they inspire their eager fans
So I may be stuck in the credits of a film
But to see an audience clap
At the end of my film, I will smile cheerfully
Nothing can make me lose that smile
And when I look back and see how far I have come
I will applaud myself for this
This poem, which entails my hopes for the future

Aashi Sharma (12)

The Other Side Of Me

I tried to hide these things,
But I know you can't hide forever.
But when these things are visible,
Nobody understands.
Every stare, every whispered word
A reflection of what you think I am.
A disability doesn't make me the person I am today
A disability is just a title.
Not all disabilities are seen.
Some live in the hidden thought,
In joints that ache without scars.
The weight of invisible battles presses harder
Because how can you explain pain
That the world refuses to believe?
Living life with these conditions,
Is a continuous fight,
Having to live this way,
Isn't fair or even right.
Living with uncertainty,
Never knowing how you'll feel,
Each day is different,
No one believes this is real.
Living with these conditions,
Is a struggle every day,
Often so overwhelming,
But we always find a way.

Isabel Nielson (17)

Sunlight

Sunlight only stretches about a quarter into the ocean,
Glimmering and glistening amongst twirling movements of colour.
Shining light on the captivating beauty,
In that which is more aesthetic than the other.

Ignorant to deep-sea fish,
Shrouded in a void of neglect.
Focusing on the 'better' ones,
It makes it easier to forget.

Portrayed as warm and saturating,
In reality, cold and darkening.
The creatures that swim in light,
And the others just watching.

Though some in the depths prefer it that way,
Losing spotlight means gaining freedom.
And some in the shallows envy the depths,
Their imperfections and movements not being focused on.

Just because they're shallow swimming,
Doesn't mean they don't feel deep.
And sometimes the ones in the depths,
Wish for a second they could be more shallow.

Emily (15)

Own Your Dream

Don't give up, don't lose your way.
Reach for the moon, shine brighter each day.
And if you miss, don't worry,
you'll find you're still among the stars, forever aligned.
Every step counts, every step's a stride.
Arise from your downfalls, let your spirit glide.
Make your move, let your dreams unfold.
Bloom in the darkness, where growth is told.
In the silence, listen to your heart.
It's beating with purpose, a brand new start.
So rise up, don't be held back.
Your time is now, let your spirit attack!

Zayan Foster (14)

I Have A Flame

All men and women are not created equal
I have a wish for all of the people
For soldiers to see the skies which are so blue
Hoping their dreams of peace come true
A brighter world for me and you
Setting their hearts ablaze
Under the sun's warming rays
With no endless battle and struggles
Instead peace replacing their troubles
Instead our happiness begins to double
Igniting a flame of peace that sets the world aglow
Together we'll build a future where love is all we know
With no endless battles and struggles
A place where we watch the stars and snuggle
Where peace will heal the endless scars
I want a gentle flame to chase away the woe
So the seeds of peace will have time to grow
With no endless battle and struggles
We'll share our dreams and unite in warm cuddles
Building a world that no war ever troubles.

Haarith Sriharan (17)

I Have A Dream Still

I have a dream
That freedom is not a fragile word,
But a song sung loud in every street,
That justice does not wait in shadows,
But walks with us in the light.

I dream of courage standing tall,
Of strength born from standing together.
I dream of brave voices, young and clear,
Saying, "We will not be silent."

I see equality written on every door,
I see respect in every hand we shake.
I see kindness chosen over cruelty,
And hope that refuses to die.

Yes, the climb is steep, the struggle long,
But I believe in the power of change.
I believe we can rise from the ashes of hate,
And shine with the fire of love.

I have a dream still,
Not just for me, but for us all.
For the world is waiting, the time is near,
To turn this dream into a life we live.

Isla Speed (12)

I Have A Dream

I have a dream
That one day all of them will come true,
I have reason to think I might scream,
But this time with joy,
A scream where no sadness nor darkness are found,
No misery nor loneliness around,
Just me and my dreams,
Where happiness is all-bound.

I had a dream,
I wish it were real,
It passed like time when scrolling through Facebook reels,
It had power,
Like Rapunzel's hair helping her escape Gothel's tower,
If it were to be true,
We wouldn't be acting like fools,
Running around without a care in the world, stupidity's whirlpool.

I have a dream,
That one day even this world,
A world with sweltering hate,
Will love, be transformed,
Into a paradise of peace, like an open door.

I have a dream,
That all of them will meet,
And darkness will be beat.

Smiles Angel Azah Som (12)

Two Worlds

A world for day -
A world for night.
Reality is close to bending.
Truth shines in the day,
While stories light the way at night.
Sagas and ideas fill your mind,
As slumber comes, and slumber goes.

At each dawn and dusk,
A world is waiting -
A world is resting,
To be heard and seen again,
Attention seekers they are,
As they call to be the loudest.
Reality always wins.

Truth and dreams,
How close yet far,
Can they truly be?
Aspiration is a beacon through the darkest truths,
And certainty is a guide through the nightmares.
But dreams can too become true,
So hope will always stay.

A world for day -
A world for night.

Reality is close to bending.
Truth shines in the day,
While stories light the way at night.

Isabella Hutchison (12)

Midnight's Angel

Blinding lights cascade, glitter sticks in my hair, I walk through fire—a loose spark hovers near my shoulder, then fades.
Heads turn, jaws drop, eyes dart—admiring desire, and I catch one glance that lingers, warm and curious.
Heels click sparks; my crown wobbles slightly,
Not chasing dreams—I let them chase me, sometimes tripping over my own rhythm, laughing.
The night bends to me; confetti flutters in sloppy arcs, drifting like tiny, trembling stars.
All eyes on me, the crowd roars—some cheer, some gasp.
Every glance ignites a flame; I feel it lick my skin, thrilling and real, like I'm both fire and wind.
Favoured by the night; I don't chase—I am the dream, messy, bold, alive—every heartbeat blazing.
And in that blaze, I leave a trail they'll never forget.

Lily Kumbhat (12)

No Space For Hate

In a world where shadows cast gloom,
Let's light a flame that will dispel the gloom
No room for hate, no space for fear,
Only love can make this crystal clear.

Bullying breaks spirits, racism divides,
Prejudice blinds and often hides
The goodness that each soul holds inside
A truth that we must now abide
Empathy's the key to open hearts,
To heal the wounds that prejudice imparts
Kindness shines a brighter light
Turning darkness into sight.

It's time to stand, to raise our voices
To choose compassion, make the choice
For every child, for every race
Where discrimination has no place.

Together, let's build a world anew
Where everyone is valued true
Ending hate begins with me and you
A future bright, inclusive, and true.

Sarah Farrukh (13)

To Dream A Dream

At night lie down to go to sleep,
And dream a dream that's yours to keep,
It can be anything, anything, anything at all,
Baking, flying or going to a ball,
My dream however,
Is very simple you see,
As I see in my mind the person I want to be,
Not a baker, not a swimmer but a dancer, oh yes!
I'm a dancer already but I want to be the best.
What is your dream? What is your hope?
It could be as simple as, being good at jump-the-rope,
Whether it's a footballer,
A cook,
A skydiver,
Or a book,
A dream is something you can do,
A dream is something that belongs to you,
A dream is something you can be,
A thought that no one else can see,
Definition by mind,
Definition by heart,
Your dreams and you are never far apart,
To dream a dream.

Felyzitee Shelley (11)

Dream Of The Vulpes Vulpes

A regal, lavish lady has me draped around her shoulders,
For my hanging form is splendid in the eyes of her beholders.
My fur is soft and silky, my eyes like gleaming pearls;
My scarlet tail contrasts so well against her flaxen curls.
I find I don't much mind it now, limp across her neck,
Living as an object, just existing to bedeck.
But no matter how I hide away my very inner soul,
I have these wistful urges I quite simply can't control:
To bound and leap and pounce around in such unbridled joy,
The way I did before entrapped and turned into a toy.
My paws had been so dirty, my maw was stained with blood,
Yet I had been so mirthful as I rolled around in mud.
When she yanks me off her nape and stuffs me in her box,
I wish I could be free again, the dream of every fox.

Clare Wilson (18)

Heaven On Earth

Heaven is a place of paradise
Earth is home
But what if Earth were a little more magical?
What if a little imagination could light a spark?
Heaven is paradise
But with a little imagination, Earth could be the same
I have a dream
Do you have a dream?
A job?
A family?
A pet?
Even a silly fantasy that you know will never actually happen?
I have a dream
My dream?
Of endless books and music
Of cosy winter nights, hot chocolate and a story
Music fading in the background
I have a dream
Some have forgotten their dreams
Or at least claim they have
Others hold on for dear life
We all have our dreams
Teamwork makes the dream work
So let's work as a team

I have a dream
So do you
Let's make our dreams a reality.

Charlotte Sacre (13)

Born Without Gold, Built With Dreams

I have a dream, bright as the rising sun,
That even the smallest steps can make the longest run.
I dream of reaching heights the world once thought too far,
To prove an ordinary soul can shine like any star.
I have a dream of breaking chains of doubt,
Of showing others what true hope is all about.
That life is not reserved for those with golden spoons,
But built with hands and hearts that reach beyond the moon.
I have a dream of laughter filling the air,
Of success not hoarded, but something we share.
To lift up families, to help others rise,
To place belief and courage in every pair of eyes.
I have a dream, and I'll hold it near,
Through every storm, through every fear.
For dreams are the bridges to all we can be,
And I dream of a world where all walk free.

Aarya Patel (16)

My Dream To Be A Writer

I dream in ink, in page and pen,
Of crafting worlds from deep within.
A quiet room, a midnight light,
I shape the dark, I birth the bright.

With every word, a voice I find,
A map that charts my restless mind.
I chase the rhythm, raw and true,
And tell the tales that won't stay blue.

I dream of books with well-worn spines,
Of readers lost between my lines.
Of tears they cry, of laughs they share,
Because I placed a moment there.

I long to touch, to move, to stir,
To turn a whisper to a blur.
Of racing hearts and turning page,
To build a truth, to speak an age.

Though doubt may knock, and silence stay,
I write the dream and dream the way.
For in this craft, both wild and free,
I write the writer I will be.

Sophie Hildebrandt (14)

The Galaxy

I had a dream
The moon cast its silver spell on me,
A vision so enchanting,
I walked toward it, advancing, dancing, prancing.
The stars like diamonds, crowned the night,
Guarding would bestow light.
The sun, in contrast with golden pride,
Painted the Earth with a radiant stride.
It danced through streets in the present glow,
While joy arose and peace did flow.
Golden streaks across the sky would chime,
Proclaiming boldly, this is my time.
The world transformed beneath the flame,
Until the moon returned to claim
Its throne above, serene, divine,
A cosmic rhyme, yours and mine.
When sunlight reigns, no shadows win,
Its warmth redeems, it cleanses sin.
I dreamed a dream, oh yes, a dream,
That changed my world, my heart, my theme.

Attalia Schultz-Nazim (12)

The Silent Sea Of Hope

We're wondering, scavenging
Searching for a place
To be free, to make noise
And do what we do best
We have the power, we have the strength
So no one can tell us no
The sheer might of a roaring wave
One that comes and is never washed away
We are a force to be reckoned with
Behold, the mighty wall
Is starting to crumble, starting to shake
On the edge of war
It's who we are, it's all within
The makings of a silent sea
Which turn and churn and
Whirl in a torpedo
Of greatness and power
And it's all ever so strange
For no one knows who we are
A mystery like the break of day
Our name is a silent sea
We are a silent breeze
And together let us bring
A thunderous flood
Brought by the silent sea.

Glory Daramola (17)

I Have A Dream

I wanted to be a poet,
to spend every ounce of euphoric life writing jubilance of words like rain pattering, drumming against my window,
but I stared too long at the page drifting out of my ink-stained palms and thought too deeply,
until even beauty began to slip away,
like Da Vinci before the ravens thou cry,
I chased meaning into luminescent shadows darkening,
casting moonlight draping across my painting,
the only glimpse of lightning spiralled endlessly until it faded and came back empty-handed,
my mind tangled in its own verse.
Now
I can't even lift a pencil,
the art I once bled for sits untouched, marinated in dust, heavy in my hands.
Perhaps madness and chaos is not the noise but the aching silence that falls when the words no longer come out...

Hafsa Hussain (12)

I Have A Dream

I have a dream so beautiful
I wish that it were true
That everyone would treat each other
Like they'd want to be treated too
No matter what the colour, religion or the race
So every person every day would wear a smilier face

I have a dream so beautiful
I wish it could be true
That there would be no pain and suffering
Or heartbreak to go through
That negativity would die
And pure love would live on
So we could be happy every day
With all the badness gone

I have a dream so beautiful
I wish it would come true
That there would be no fear in life
Or hate for me and you
For future generations
Their skies forever will be blue

I have a dream so beautiful
Help me to make it true.

Athena Pointon (12)

A World Of Unity

I have a dream of a world so fair,
Where love and kindness fill the air.
Where differences make us strong and bright,
And unity shines with all its light.

In this world, compassion is the key,
And kindness is the way we live with glee.
No one's left out, no one's blue,
We're all connected, through and through.

I dream of a place where love does abide,
Where everyone's valued and everyone's inside.
No walls to keep us apart, no hate to share,
Just hearts that beat as one, with love to spare.

Let's build this world, let's make it real,
A place where love and kindness are the way we feel.
I have a dream, and I think you do too,
Let's make it happen, let's see it through!

Hammad Farrukh (12)

We Are One

I slept, I tossed, I turned.
The sand of hope tickled my feet,
Knowing that what storms come and go
We are one and won't accept defeat.
In times of sunshine, we wear a smile
It is the positivity that makes it worthwhile
To embrace the opportunities that we see,
And glide with the motion at our own liberty.
Yet we ignore the haters, the ones who try
To shoot and cut us deep with their words.
Unlike them, we rise high and strong
As we zap them with what the truth hurts.
We are one, we are our own leaders:
As well as achievers and pure believers,
Who work for our dream the night through
As we accept those who support our dreams
Because in the end, we'll dance along
As we are us, we are one.

Jake L. Palmer (16)

Dream Free

I have a dream to be a swimmer
An Olympic medal winner.
In the pool I'll finish first
Or even outside I'll be far from worst.
I have a dream to be a physiotherapist.
To help people's injuries as I get the gist.
Even if I'm not a swimmer, I can help those with their dream career
Getting them to be able to be at peak performance and without injury fear.
I have a dream to travel worldwide
To see what the world has to hide
To explore how other people live
And help them out with whatever I can give.
I have a dream to be me
And be truly free
To do what I want to do
And like whoever, too.
So Martin Luther King, thank you
You helped many black people to dream for the first time too.

Vincent Hennessy-Price (13)

Nobody Hears The Rainforest's Cry...

Under the canopy, the place is alive,
Animals pleading us to survive.
Trees, still like basins, holding in rain,
The rainforest is everything but plain.
Suddenly, everything is demolished, all dreams,
And pollution works its way into the streams.
What used to be a pulchritudinous thing,
Turns into an excruciating sting.
We are the monsters, cutting homes down,
Only so that we own the crown.
We fill the forest with fright,
Resulting in our delight.
Yet if we throw unused paper away,
Growth of nature will delay.
We will never bring back what it was before,
The only thing we can do is explore.
Nobody hears the rainforest's cry
As it slowly perishes, leaving only the sky...

Alice Teatino (12)

I Wish

I wish for a place of peace and love,
For a place we all belong,
A place so sought after
Where nothing could go wrong.

I wish for a place so full of happiness,
For a place so full of joy,
For a place that gives equality
To every girl and boy.

I wish for a place where there is no war,
For a place where everyone can be,
For a place with freedom for all,
A place for you and me.

I wish for a place with no wickedness,
For a place where everyone is kind,
For a place that accepts everybody,
A place to speak your mind.

I wish for a place like this,
I think of it every day,
I sit and think to myself,
"Why can't Earth be this way?"

Evie Barrett (13)

Rewrite The Seam

I have a dream
To change the world
Rewrite the seam
Come together, as one united team
Where everyone has enough
No one has to live in the rough
Everyone has shelter, a good home
No one is told to go back to where they come from
This is my dream, I shout it aloud
Let's make a world, of which we can all be proud
A world founded on fairness, with every person a kind heart
Throwing open each window, letting new journeys start
Where everyone has enough to thrive
We all have better lives
Everyone has shelter, a place called home
No one is told to leave or roam
This is my dream—I shall rewrite the seam
I shout it loud:
Let's build a world that makes us proud...

Robyn Blissett-Barlow (13)

We All Have A Dream

We all have dreams
Women have dreams.
Yes, we all did
But because the world was full of men, away they hid
Perhaps women want to be politicians
We have wonderful intuition
I have a dream to become a writer
Mary Ann Evan had the gasoline and the lighter
To set the world ablaze with her stories so brave
Credits given to men, credits we crave
Every woman stares down at us
Telling us to draft our stories even if that means causing a fuss
I want to dream just like men do
I had a dream when I was younger
To become a baker, feeding the hunger
I still dream of that, but also draft books,
But men force ideology that they are majestic rivers, and we, the women, are brooks.

Skylar Jolly (12)

My Endless Dreams Through Outerspace

I have a dream,
That feels like a light beam.
Small and imaginable to the outside world,
But big and bold to the inside girl.

Time to let my colours show
Into the endless unknown.
As ideas cripple and curl
My world starts to swirl and twirl.

Helmets, suits and rocketships,
I hope to one day fly into the abyss.
Floating and jumping on the moon,
I hope I don't lose a boot!

How I wish to meet MY world
And see MY dreams come true,
Although I have a science test due.
Lights flicker and glass shatters,
But I can feel the platters.

Daydreams and late thoughts,
Could come after all.
You never know what could fall through.

Amelia Barton (12)

Carpe Diem

I long for my voice to find its place,
In melody, story, or rhyme's embrace,
I seek only to leave a trace.

To have my tales told would be a dream,
The thought of people looking up to me,
Because my words allow them to finally feel free.

Whether my fantasies will ever come true,
I guess I'll leave that up to you,
And hope that this lucid of mine will be my debut.

This is my form of self-expression,
And it pains me to see others live lives in quiet desperation,
When freedom is created in just a spark of imagination.

Why let silence seal your hearse,
When your voice can break the curse,
So do tell me—what will be your verse?

Bronwyn Hyland (14)

Echoes Of The Past: I Have A Dream

Suffering. Timeless misery. A past only time will tell.

I have a dream, a dream to become a historian and
discover the ruins of the past—whether it's heartbreaking,
inhumane or worse.

History, you can unearth parts of your heritage you'd never
know,
You can go through time with a flow,
Parts of centuries, you can learn a lot,
But don't get your facts in a knot,
Locate sources from years ago,
Make sure to preserve them so they don't blow.

Denude crimes from the past,
Remember to make it last.

You can learn a lot from history,
Some are still a mystery.

Suffering. Timeless misery. A past only time will tell.

Mia Garratt (12)

Dreams That Define Me

I have a dream, a vision of fire,
A heart that is burning with endless desire.
I have a dream to command the law,
A shield for the weak, a voice that will roar.
I have a dream to dance with the skies,
To move like the lightning, to dazzle all eyes.
I have a dream for wisdom untold,
A mind like a diamond, unbreakable, bold.
I have a dream that hate will decay,
Like shadows that vanish at break of day.
I have a dream of learning supreme,
Each book is a mountain, each lesson a beam.
I have a dream—unshaken, bright,
The sunrise that scatters the darkness of night.
For dreams are the arrows, and I am the bow,
They carry me forward, they help me to grow.

Tahlia Crossgill (12)

I Have A Dream

I had a dream once
I was flying through the clear blue sky
It was surreal
When a wizard appeared
Wearing all blue apart from his hat
Orange top hat he wore
He wasn't any old wizard
He was small with green hair
With a glare
So rare
It hypnotised me
He shared his advice
Never go near the apple tree
"What's so wrong with it?" I exclaimed
"It looks like any old tree"
He began with a strange rhythm
Apples, do they have a meaning?
You're dreaming, right?
Flight is your aim
Flames are red
Apples are red
Beds right there
Which is fair
Do you want to know something?
Nothing has meaning.

Liara Ronan (12)

The Dream On The Court

I have a dream of lights that gleam,
Crowds that rise, and voices that scream.
The ball in my hands, the shot in the air,
A moment of glory, a future so rare.

I have a dream of sweat and grind,
Late-night drills and a focused mind.
From cracked-up courts to arenas bright,
Turning each struggle into my flight.

I have a dream of breaking the chains,
Proving my worth through losses and gains.
To inspire the kids who feel too small,
That with heart and hustle, they can stand tall.

I have a dream-my name in the game,
But more than the trophies, more than the fame:
To leave a mark, to spark belief,
That dreams can rise above all grief.

Garbi Animola (13)

Five, Six, Seven, Eight

I have a dream.
Five, six, seven, eight twirls around my brain,
lingering day in, day out.
Through every rhythm I dance;
it's like an electric connection flowing from my brain
all the way down to my toes.
When I dance, the only thing I'm focused on is dance.
The room goes quiet, and my heart takes flight;
like a plane when it's setting off.
I put the world on pause as the music carries on playing.
As I count the steps they stir in my mind,
creating a spark of light.
I breathe through the shadows and shine through dance.
My light roars; a melody feels the air.
Each spin, each leap a whispered prayer.
Bold and free.
I have a dream.

Kenzie Paisley-Nyarko (12)

Our World

Our world is strong,
our world is powerful.
But slowly, slowly,
the air is becoming coaly.

Our world is strong,
our world is powerful.
Our trees are dying,
the land is drying.

Our world is strong,
our world is powerful.
Our animals are becoming extinct,
all that are distinct.

Our world is strong,
our world is powerful.
Climate change is increasing,
and money isn't decreasing.

Our world is strong,
our world is powerful.
Countries won't make peace,
when will it cease?

Our world is strong,
our world is powerful.
We can fix this all,
if we work together.

Lily Merany (12)

Hope Hurl

Hopes and dreams I eat for breakfast,
yet I puke it up by lunch.
They're splattered across the floor.
Spreading under my feet.
There's chunks of sacrifice, and globs of defeat.
Yet the acidic base of the future, glistens in the light.
Reflecting my image unto it.
I see myself in five years, right betwixt the piece of determination.
He's smiling happily back at me.
We make eye contact and hold it for a while.
My face is sour and upset.
Dirty and marked.
I kneel to the ground, and clean up the mess I've made.
This time lighter and more prepared than before.
I think I can hold it down this time,
or at least I'll try.

Max Shelton (16)

I Had A Vision

I had a vision that,
People on Earth would be,
Living in harmony,
Melodies capturing,
Culturing mem'ries of,
Sweet-stricken sympathies,
Bloomed into symphonies,
But it did not.

'Stead we have hate and anger,
'Stead we have revenge and disaster,
'Stead we have politics and war,
'Stead we store contempt, and abhor each other.

I have a vision see,
People on Earth will be,
Living in harmony,
Capturing melodies,
Culturing mem'ries of,
Sweet-striking sympathies,
Blooming to symphonies,
Creating a world to be

Loved, to be equal.
Creating a world to be,
Home...

Aaron Flynn (16)

Black Pearl

Black is something you can't take back
Black is something others may lack
Black can be good
Black can be bad
Black is something that makes people mad
Listen,
Black is something that can change the world
Black can be as beautiful as a pearl
Black can be perfection
Black is apparent to have intentions
Black can never have peace at a reservation
Black is shown to be a nasty mutation
Black is something that never gets respect
Black always gets so much neglect
Black should be treated even better
Police arrest an idol just because of a letter
Black and white, all of this could be done
If we fight together, we can be one!

Olumide Tyson Williams (12)

I Have A Dream

In my heart, a fire ignites,
A vision to support and lift every light,
To mentor, look after, and guide,
And be a teacher always by their side.

My aspiration glows, an unchanging flame,
To settle in young hearts hope's name,
To build them a future where they soar,
And open wide with each challenging door.

With every barrier, I stay true,
To make an impact, to see them through,
To listen, help, and always care,
And show them love is always there.

This is my dream, my leading star,
To be a teacher, close or far,
To help them develop, make them strong,
And turn their dreams into one lifelong happy song.

Demi Lewis (16)

My Wish

I wish for all violence in this world to go away and that
everyone can be at peace, and just simply get along.
I wish that all the animals that are currently getting
treated badly get the help they deserve, and start to
receive love instead of punishments.
I wish that people could treat each other how they would
want to be treated instead of being horrible to each other;
after all, we are all human, we have feelings!
I wish that learning would come easier to those who
struggle to learn due to learning disabilities or any other
kind of disabilities and get treated like how others would
want to be treated and not like they are completely
incapable of doing anything on their own!

Mia Utting (13)

Whispers Through Time

Years go by like flicking through a book.
Each page documenting a good memory.
Maybe a picture you once took.
Or the name of your favourite melody.

Some days are bright and full of life.
Where laughter echoes in the breeze.
We find the power among the strife.
So happiness would never cease.

Though times could be tough sometimes.
And it's hard to find the light.
Our eyes still blink in silent chimes.
Through every sleepless night.

So I dream to hold on to joy all life long.
To appreciate what life delivers.
Through every hardship, fierce and long.
I'll stand up and flow with the rivers.

Mennah Elbarbary (12)

I Have A Dream

I have a dream...
I have a dream that one day I will be a cricketer.
A dream where I proudly stand and see people cheering for me.
I have a dream that one day I will represent my country at a big level.
A dream where I make my country proud of me.
I have a dream that one day I will lift the World Cup trophy.
A dream where I get to hold the prestigious trophy in my bare hands.
I have a dream that one day I will be a successful cricketer.
A dream where I can stand on my feet with pride.
I have a dream that one day I will be a wonderful man.
A dream where I can make my family feel honoured and where I can help others pursue their dreams.

Abheer Shetty (12)

My Dream

To float through space, no thought in mind
Embodied with grace, no sense of time
To bloom like a flower, lush and bright
Lost in thought for hours, no disturbance in sight
To portray a deer, a peaceful being
Prance on and on, a freeing feeling
To finish your show, in front of many
An ethereal glow, for the next, you're ready
To experience pride, from completing your piece
Fireworks inside, the moment should never cease
All these emotions, metaphors too
Put dreams in motion, believe they'll come true
I want to dance before thousands, illuminating the stage
It could soon be ours, my dream, not the last page.

Meena Sathyendra (13)

The Calling Of The Curious Heart

Within the pulse of life's mysterious art,
where cells and coded whispers softly sing,
I feel a yearning rise within my heart,
to walk the path where truth and wonder cling.

The microscope reveals a secret glow,
each strand of DNA a quiet rhyme;
through blood and breath, the hidden patterns show
the poetry of flesh, the dance of time.

To heal, to learn, to question and to find,
to turn uncertainty to steady light,
this noble craft ignites both soul and mind,
a beacon shining through the endless night.

O science, let me serve your boundless quest,
and place my eager heart within your test.

Daisy Jane Gibbons (13)

No Freedom Here

No freedom here,
In this land of despair.
These horrible walls, never free,
Every day we struggle, but we just need to be heard.
Our voices are silenced,
Black cloths unwillingly wrapped around our faces,
Threatening to kill us,
If we ever try to speak.
No freedom here,
Our education has been destroyed,
But we are 'just girls',
And we 'need to learn'.
Here on this demoralised no-man's land,
We are left stranded.
Dancing in disdain,
Until the men can come and stab us, causing stains.
No freedom here, I wish it were different,
But unfortunately,
Not everyone can win.

Daria Nuta (12)

I Have A Dream...

I have a dream but it's not what you think,
I have a dream, and it's lined in rose pink,
It's not hard but it definitely seems so,
I would try and try but it could never show,

Beyond others and through the crowd,
If true, I would stand up proud,
I wish this dream could be mine,
If it were, I'd be on cloud nine,

I have a dream but it's not what you think,
I have a dream which many overthink,
Why can't I do it?
Why, why, why?

My dream is not what you think,
My dream is to be done in a blink,
My dream is to be free,
My dream is to be me.

Aarudhraa Premnath (13)

One Can Dream

Willow, who wanted to dance on the Broadway stage,
was told by her mother, "One can dream."
Evan, who wanted to be a football player for Liverpool FC,
was told, "One can dream."
Lilly, who wanted to be a singer at the French opera,
was told, "One can dream."
Raven, on the other hand, wanted to be a netball player
and was told, "One can do it."
Ellanna, who wanted to be a zoologist,
was told, "The stars are the limit for you, kid."
The moral of the poem is
perhaps it's not the kids who are not ambitious,
perhaps it's the parents crushing their children.

Layla Morris (12)

I Have A Dream

I have a dream of brighter skies,
Where hope is seen in every eye,
Where rivers run both clean and free,
And hearts are bound by unity.

I have a dream that hands will meet,
Across all borders, every street,
That voices rise, both strong and true,
And justice wears no tinted hue.

I have a dream of kinder days,
Where children laugh in endless ways,
Where walls of fear are torn apart,
And love is written on each heart.

I have a dream the world will find,
The strength of soul, the peace of mind,
And step by step, through dark or gleam,
We'll walk together toward the dream.

AJ Vallis (14)

The Silenced Voices

I have a dream for the voices that have been silenced.
I wish for them all to be heard,
So then everyone can finally learn,
I wish the silenced had the courage
To shout out their problems,
So the world can finally be encouraged,
To help undo that permanent damage,
Looking the other way has caused,
I need the silenced to know that they aren't the lost cause,
To put this world that has strayed back on the right road,
I want the silenced to shatter loud.
So they can tell us the pain they've endured
All I have is this one dream,
To make the silenced as loud as they should've always been.

Tharuki Jayasundara (13)

A Dream From Under The Rubble

I have a dream,
For Palestine to be free,
Oh, please be okay,
Help is on the way,
Your souls under the rubble, we hear your screams,
Please world, let them be free,
Children of Gaza, your smiles shine,
Parents of Gaza, you're just so kind,
We understand, your pain and struggle,
Your suffer and fear is kept in a bubble,
No food and drink, you've hit starvation,
Yet you're still here, with your amazing imagination,
Smoke everywhere, fire burning,
But the world here still isn't learning,
So let them be okay,
Let them be free,
I have a dream for Palestine to be free!

Maryam Hansrod (12)

An Author's Dream

I have a dream.
I want to soar high up in the clouds.
I want to discover the depths of the sea.
I want to feel my feet on the ground.
I want to fall into worlds they call free.
I want my words to be like portals.
I want to know what we could be.
I want to hear stories of new mortals.
I want people to journey with me.
I want to create a picture in your mind.
I want to watch it grow.
I want to create a mystical kind.
I want to make it a show.
I want to make dreams and light fires.
I want to spark something new.
I want to twist a tale like brier.
I want to see a breakthrough.

Autumn-Rae Carter (13)

Different Daunting Dreams

I have a dream.
One where the stars are sewn in the dark sky.
One where I can gather their light from up high.

I have a dream.
One where the dandelions take flight,
And turn into kites,
To brush away the night.
One where plants grow tall,
And seeds are shaped like basketballs.

I have a dream.
One where I can hug strangers,
And befriend the universe.
One where individuals become groups,
And we help each other make roots.

I have a dream where people's ears are pointy,
Like elves and fairies.
So that we live just like them,
We live in harmony.

Latifah Kabore (13)

Dreams

Dreams, dreams, dreams,
Shattered dreams,
Future dreams,
Fading dreams,
Hopeful dreams,
It's good to dream,
It's good to gleam,
It's good to be enough,
It's good to love,
Dreaming is to feel accepted,
Dreaming is to feel protected,
Dreaming is to feel seen,
Dreaming is to feel serene,
Sometimes you cry,
Sometimes you fly,
Sometimes you flail,
Sometimes you exhale,
Dreaming is like lying on a cloud,
Dreaming is as scary as being bound,
Dreaming is like a warm, soft hug,
Dreaming is as if life gave a tug,
Dreams, dreams, dreams.

Rossa Brown (12)

Night Vision

The night has fallen, the moon is shining, your eyes are shut but your mind is exploring.
The clouds have vanished, the secrets of dreams have been revealed.
As night visions arrive, the darkness will fade and light will win once again.
You shall rule over your own dreams, wishes or even desires.
What you hold most in your heart shall come visit your dreams and take over.
The world has not yet seen this brilliant mind because you must keep your identity a secret.
Dreams are lanterns in the night, flickering with a secret light and they guide us through the nightmares.
What shall come to visit your mind tonight?

Aminah Shah (13)

Journeys Of A Dreamer

Beneath a sky of endless gold
Lies a dream so big and bold
Drifts the winds and kisses the breeze
Water drips and bounces on trees.

Aromas of spices and fresh bread
Guide me along trails ahead
The countless stars gleaming bright
Lead me gently through the night.

I'll glide through boundless seas
Unlocking doors with priceless keys
And every stream will call my name
Achieving both my goal, my aim.

I'll travel the world both near and far
Unleashing wonders wherever they are
Across the world, where freedom flows
This was the day my dream arose.

Salma Elbarbary (14)

My Dreams In The Future

My dreams for the future are to be:
Singer.
Dancer.
Actor.
Artist.
Gamer.
Anime streamer.
Fashion designer.
Designer.
Decorator.

I think these are really good achievements to want to do and I think that I will be one of these at some point in life if I just put my mind to it and I think that if I work hard enough in school and I teach myself at home too, I think I can achieve one of these. I really like doing these activities quite a lot because they are really fun to do. I'm leaning towards doing designing or decorating because I really enjoy designing and decorating things.

Kasey-Leigh Lloyd (12)

My Dream

I had a dream
That I lived in the world of books
I had high self-esteem
And I had perfect looks
I dreamt of being a spy
I dreamt of fighting dragons
I dreamt of flying in the sky
With a constant happy expression
However, I woke up
And reality met my eyes
My dreams were made up
And reality took me by surprise
Fiction isn't real
Nor are the pages of books
Sadness is what people feel
The streets are full of crooks
But I had books to assist me
And my dream became clear
I would be the author I always could be
And rid my readers of their fear.

Simrina Bhachu (13)

The Shape Of Absence In Love

A ges erode the warmth once held close,
B eneath the weight of silence, promises fall,
S hadows lengthen where laughter used to be,
E mptiness echoes in the halls,
N ight gathers where dawn should call.
C old winds whisper forgotten names,
E ternity swallows the dying flames.

I n the quiet, memories stir,
N ow a ghost of what we were.

L ost is the touch, the whispered word,
O blivion's embrace, forever heard.
V oid remains where love took flight,
E choes fade into the lonely night.

Mya Thompson (13)

Learn To Fly

I am a bird
One who can't fly
My feathers rubbed raw from the woven rope
That binds me and strips me from freedom
The freedom I see all around me;
Oh, the doves clasping olive branches in their beaks
And spreading their glistening wings in the sun
Oh, the seagulls free to squawk and caw to the sea
And feel the harsh wind against their feathers
But the woven rope that binds me will not relent
And see what of the world I am missing
Because I am a bird
One who can't fly
But when they free me of my binds I will be free
And I will learn to fly.

Amaya-Rose Tapper (14)

I Have A Dream

I have a dream,
that one day I will be on the newspaper, holding an award,
that I won a scholarship to one of the best universities,
but will that ever happen?
Will my dream ever come true?
Will I lose all hope?
My mum always told me that dreams do come true
if I put in the work and effort.
But I think she is only saying that because I'm her daughter.
Look at me in a foreign land, a place I want to call home,
imagine if I become well-known all around the world,
that's a special dream.
A dream I forever have, and a dream I will forever cherish.

Winifred Chinazam Ubah (12)

I Have A Dream

Deforestation,
Desertification,
Erosion, and
Extinction;
I stood on the bare and sandy land with desperation,
I could only see logs, smoke and factories,
The rivers were choked by plastic bottles.
The air was burdened with smog and fumes.
I woke from a nightmare.
But this is not what I dream for.
I dream of forests prospering again,
I dream of water flowing clear,
I dream of air refreshing everywhere,
I dream of a world where all types of animals will be safe and loved,
With no more species that will disappear.
I have a dream.

Ruixi Bai (12)

If I Had A Dream

If I had a dream
I would run through the airs of utopia
Play games with birds and butterflies
Meet my idols and favourite writers
Dance through gardens of flowers
Feel the grass shimmer on my feet
Feel the tan on my skin
Shimmering and showing

If I had a dream
I would feel peace in my eyes
Play football with legends
Meet presidents and prime ministers
Sing in front of crowds
Pet lions and tigers
Learn all history and music
Interesting and soothing

If I had a dream,
If I had a dream...

Patrick Sloan (12)

My Thousand Dreams

In my thousand dreams,
I'm here, reading and writing,
Playing, dancing,
Swirling about.
Happy as a bird in a berry bush.
Where no worries that conceal my happiness,
Where I can lie in grass and smell the freshness in the clean air.
Where I can spend hours at a time playing with Holly, my supernoodle supermodel,
Where I can cuddle with my Tobi dog,
Or where I curl up in bed all day,
Where I crochet all day, and buy as much yarn as I desire,
Where I could be with my family,
Where I could learn and,
Where I could craft.
Where I could be,
Me,
That's my thousand dreams.

Philippa Barratt (11)

A Broken Prophecy

In twilight's grasp, where shadows roam,
A dream unfolds, stemmed from home.
A prophecy whispers, old as time,
Now shattered fragments, lost in vines.

Through clouds of fog—a future gleamed,
A world restored; a world redeemed.
But the broken prophecy had other plans,
As the future slipped from our hero's hands...

A prophecy once new: now turned to dust,
Shines a broken promise, and fading trust.
In this dream—a desperate plea,
The echo of screams; wishing to be free.

For the broken prophecy can't guarantee,
A world of glee,
Or a world to flee?

Jessica Dane (14)

A Dream Is But A Dream

I have a dream,
Where we could all gleam,
Like the stars and the moon in the sky.

I have a dream,
Where people are seen,
And no one is just passing by.

I have a dream,
Where there's equality,
And no one is above another.

I have a dream,
Where everyone's friendly,
And no one judges the other.

I have a dream,
Where I could be me,
And happiness is all I would feel.

I have a dream,
But it just seems,
That none of this could ever be real.

Louise Owen (14)

Playing Through The Ages

Tag! You're it!
Come and chase me around the tree
That was acceptable to play when I was only three
Stack the Lego
Make a tower!
I'll go grab more bricks
I enjoyed all that while I was innocent and six
Oi! Where are you going with that?
The strawberry elephant is mine!
Playing Roblox Steal a Brainrot
Was all I did when I was nine
FALL BACK!!! They're killing us!!
Sniper them, work as a team!
Online shooting games are all you're supposed to play
Now you're thirteen.

Gwen Anscombe (13)

Tiptoes

My tiptoes fold before my body does
Crashing against the floor like a meteor mating with Earth.
An unlucky shooting star. Pointless.
My silhouette still stood
Running the rings of Saturn, I'm racing the idea of being last
My mirror competitors
On the very edge, I'm black and blue. My hand strained reaching for stars.
An exasperated entity
Full of empty, yet overflowing and drowned
The thorns itch my palm, I drop, red ribbon rolls out my fingertips
Did I disappoint you, or does this mean I win?

Tilly Green Harper (15)

I Have A Dream

I have a dream, I have a dream,
Where I can have a peaceful life,
Without conflict and war,
And without killing and kidnapping,
As we are brothers and sisters,
Let us live as one and be kind,
Love one another and be caring,
Be each other's keeper in times of trouble,
Be each other's comforter and best friend,
Listen to each other's problems,
And find a way to solve it,
Or cheer them up so they will be happy,
That's what I dream of,
I hope one day it will happen.

Joshua John-Isaac (14)

Black: A Colour Or An Answer?

Black, a colour or an answer?
Every stare, every glare, every flare.
Black, black, black.
Expected to be tamed, always ashamed.
The bright inside must deny the fight.
Black, black, black.
Depressed, suppressed, oppressed,
Everywhere, anywhere, always there.
Black, black, black.
A stage filled with grace, a shadow that must be shown a light.
Black, black, black.
Equal rights? Black lives? Defined minds?
A colour or an answer.
Black, black, black.
I have a dream.

Chelsea Iyoha (17)

One Pathway

Going to bed every night,
Wishing for the same thing,
Dreaming what could be mine.
My own office,
Books full of creativity,
Fashion full of unique imagination.
Walking down the catwalk,
Cameras flashing at your every movement,
Different outfits on every walk.
Offers that could change your life,
From being an unknown girl,
To being the world's most famous fashion icon.
Money doesn't define you,
But your future could,
I have a dream and this is mine.

Leah Morris (13)

Make Your Mark

I have a dream!
I stand here today
With a say,
I may be small
But the world is held
In our hands,
You may not agree
But everyone is here,
Some with fear,
Don't cry another tear,
Everyone needs rights,
No matter if you can't write!
The joy of being part of changing the world,
No matter who you are,
You are the start,
So make your mark,
Come on, don't laugh,
Everyone needs rights,
No matter if you can't write!

Amelia Bailey (13)

YoungWriters Est. 1991

I Have A Dream

I have a dream,
From when I was small,
To become an artist,
And sell to all.

I'll open a shop,
And people shall come,
They'll tell me what they want,
And I'll draw it by thumb.

I can do it on the tablet,
A picture to a cartoon,
I spend all day drawing it,
And listen to an amazing tune.

Although I'm told I can't,
I believe I can do it,
Already I can draw,
So I can make big money with it.

Lily Brown (12)

My Dream

For Cara

I have a dream I hope to come true
I want to stay all my life with you
My dream is to be there for you
For us to stick together just like glue
But there's nothing that I could ever say
To sum up how much I love you each day
My heart beats so very fast
When I see you smile and laugh
To explain how much you mean to me
To show how you make me full of glee
I really hope my dream will come true
Because I really, really do love you.

Megan Roberts (14)

Soaring High

I have a dream that one day love will be soaring high through the skies,
Looking down at the crowds, waving them on.
I have a dream that she will look to her left and see women flying side by side her.
She dreams that she will serve her country in her jet.
I dream that little girls will be able to dream about being a pilot,
That she can look at the Red Arrows and think about joining.
I dream that one day I will be in the RAF.

Ivy Bradshaw (13)

I Have A Dream About This World

I have a dream,
and it's not what it seems.
I want the world to be better,
where no one will write a complaint letter.
I want it to be fun,
where everyone will happily run.
With no bills,
and no one ever kills.
Where no one makes fun of people for who they are,
and they can be called a star.
Where people don't get judged,
or misjudged.
I want a better world,
like the nether world.

Esmay Jackson (12)

Law

Law is a way to be the voice for the voiceless
Law is the part where you show some confidence
Law is the dream God put in my heart
Law is the job that I will soon start
Law is a woman, or that's what they say
Law is the point where it's time to stop running away
Law is when looks and justice are served
Law is when you're born to fight for justice
This is my story so it's time to embrace yours.

Saanvi Bolisetty (12)

My Favourite Dream

I'll jump from a plane
With these large wings on my back
I'd be soaring high
I'd never look back
With the soft wind in my hair
I could touch the clouds
And as I descend
I would land in the blue sea
Swim with the dolphins
Happy as can be
I could even get ice cream
And do this with friends
That would be my dream
I'd hope it never would end
My favourite dream.

Aayan Zehra Madani (12)

Just You?

I don't have a dream. Do I?
I guess that I wish, and oh, I can only wish
That everyone saw the world like I do.
Naturally, one thinks of their personal life...
Is that all a dream is?
A dream that only includes you.
What about the distressed?
Starvation, disorder, disease.
Those who live in fear,
Poverty, illness, fatality.
If only everyone saw the world like I do.
That is my dream.

Maryam Iqbal (13)

Wonders And Dreams

Space stretches without end
A dream painted in stars and silence,
Galaxies turn like timeless storms,
And wonder fills the dark.
Mystery hums through the night,
A world of silence whispers.
The heart of the universe,
The silence of the skies,
Holds secrets swirling down black holes.
A dream of endless wonder,
Where we awaken in light.
Carried by the sea of enigma.

Maxine Meyerowitz Singh (12)

My Recurring Dream

I had a dream last night,
It wasn't a nightmare,
But it wasn't a good dream.
I dreamt I was happy,
I dreamt I was smart,
I dreamt I felt beautiful,
I dreamt I felt confident in my own body,
I dreamt I was comfortable with my sexuality,
And, I dreamt that one day I could wake up
And that could all become a reality.
But, do dreams ever come true?

Mya Jones (14)

To Help Animals

I have a dream, that one day all animals will be safe,
All safe and sound in their bed, no worries to think about,
Animal testing businesses have reasons, but are they worth a life for it not to work?
Does the scream of desperate escape not worry you when the end of your days has been lived?
That you would go to hell!
Stop animal crime before it's too late.

Olivia Hart (12)

A Big Dream

A breath of fresh air to flow through my lungs
That has not been polluted,
For a tree as high as the sky to hold me
That has not fallen,
For a government to regulate power
That has not been corrupt,
For my heart to be completely whole
That has not broken,
To gasp for air emerging from salty seas
That has not been polluted.

Ashleigh Fieldhouse (16)

I Have A Dream

I have a dream to stop homelessness,
The thought of it makes me want to weep.
I have a dream, the thought of loneliness of the biting air
and the thought of hopelessness and despair.
Do you ever feel regret that you have too much?
So, please never forget. Help, before it's too late.

Eloise Bailey (13)

Imaginary Hell

Bang bullets bang
Run rabbits run
Bleed woman bleed
Pads.
Cost.
Money.
Drop bombs drop
Bang bullets bang
We sit here without a care
Knowing people are hurt elsewhere
In the end, it's all just a dictator's dream
Or is it just Earth reality?

Florence Desyllas (16)

My Reverie

My reverie is the safest place.
All my thoughts in deep space.
All my dreams full of glee.
All my dreams make you feel free.
In my dreams, nobody insecure.
In my dreams, all sweet and pure.
Outside of my dreams, fear and fright.
Outside of my dreams, tears and fight.

Gurupartap Dhillon (13)

To Be A Footballer

I dream of playing for England and being the best in the world
But my friend Neil, his finger was curled
On the pitch I play
I play all day
I dream to play for Manchester United
I wish to fight it
My kit is green and blue and red
I wish I could go to bed.

Aidann Parkinson (13)

Peace

I have a dream that's calm like a stream, its water is still as ice.
The land was filled with an atmosphere of air that you want to breathe.
The trees give plenty that help us in our needs.
The birds in the nest chirp and fish swim as they please.
That was my dream.

Paul Reddy Thokkudubiyyapu (13)

Dare To Dream

D are to dream, for
R acism to be obliterated, for
E quality to be established through education and clean
  hearts,
A nd so, to achieve humanity and peace for centuries to
  come, a
M ulticultural world that brings tranquillity.

Siyana Safa Khalique (12)

I Will Make It Happen

I had a dream,
To wear the badge with pride,
To rise through the ranks,
The highest of the highest,
A name that stands for justice

I had a dream,
To make my parents proud,
To build my reputation,
To grow in strength and wisdom.

Syeda Anisa Mumtaz Nakvi (12)

I Have A Dream

D eep in the night, a candle glows,
R ising with hope as freedom grows,
E very child singing their voices strong,
A nation united where all belong,
M arching together we carry the flame.

Manel Benmessahel (12)